REVOLT
on the Campus

M. STANTON EVANS

Chicago 1961

HENRY REGNERY COMPANY

Acknowledgments

I SHOULD LIKE to acknowledge the very real and material contributions of a number of people who assisted in various phases of the preparation of this essay. First and foremost, for extensive and patient help in reading and checking the manuscript, Miss Sue Ellen Moore. For supplying data and suggesting corrections in the text, Allan Ryskind, Robert Croll, and William Schulz. For typing and related tasks, my assistant, Miss Josephine Mohr, and Mrs. Amanda Dell. For continued counsel on the folkways of young conservatives, Don Lipsett. And for providing the index, Mr. and Mrs. Lawrence Arany.

For My Parents

Preface

HISTORIANS MAY WELL record the decade of the 1960's as the era in which conservatism, as a viable political force, finally came into its own. This may appear to be an overly optimistic judgment, since conservatism has been all but silent on the national political scene for some time. But events of the past few years, particularly among college students, are signalling the birth of a movement which promises to rescue the United States from her past few decades of debilitating indecision and frightening loss of direction.

Perhaps no other generation has been the subject of so much critical study, so much social probing, as this one. Professional writers, educators, corporate executives, sociologists and psychologists—all have taken the pulse of modern America and have found it feeble. Yet, while those diagnosticians—occupying every conceivable point on the ideological and political compass—generally have been accurate in their evaluation of the problem, most of them, including those whose diagnoses have climbed onto the best seller charts, have overlooked or ignored the causes of our national malady.

It is precisely these causes toward which, among other things, M. Stanton Evans turns his attention. Both from his vantage point within the academy, from which he recently emerged after making a brilliant record, and within the world of daily newspapers, where he currently applies his talents as editor of *The Indianapolis News,* he finds our nation beset by the Four Horsemen of contemporary Liberalism: statism, with its worship of the collective; permissiveness, with its denial of absolute standards of value; egalitarianism, by means of which everyone is reduced to the lowest common denominator; and adjustment, our eagerness to achieve group harmony at the expense of individuality.

But Stan Evans is far from discouraged. For he finds, spawned in the heartland of Liberalism, within the college itself, a renascent conservatism, dedicated to the wisdom of our ancestors and to the verities which ever have existed to guide fallible man on his perilous, often discouraging, journey through the ages. "It is the Liberal who is old—who has aged in the comfortable exercise of power," writes Evans, "and it is the conservative who is young, angry, declassé."

And so it is. Happily, even in our age of modulation, when loyalties and principles seem too often in disgrace with fortune and in men's eyes, this dynamic new force is raising its voice more loudly and clearly than many of us dreamed possible. And in the background, one hears the strains of Liberalism's Götterdämmerung, the swan song of an enervated ideology which was tried and found sadly wanting.

There is one glaring omission in the book which, in fairness to its author and readers, should be noted. In describing the intellectuals who are in the vanguard of the conservative movement, the author omitted mention of one of the most brilliant of them all—himself. Already, at the age of twenty-seven, Stan Evans has established himself as one of conservatism's leading thinkers and writers, and his star is certain to wax even brighter with time. He, as well as any single person, epitomizes the intelligence, the vigor, and the depth of the conservative revival. And, secure in the knowledge that the future belongs to him and to the many other young people mentioned in this book, I rejoice knowing that the nation will be in good hands.

EUGENE C. PULLIAM
PUBLISHER
The Indianapolis News

CONTENTS

Introductory:
A Memoir

"INDIVIDUALISM IS DYING AT YALE, and without a fight." That was Bill Buckley's somber conclusion in his 1951 bestseller, *God and Man at Yale*. And I can testify that, as of that year, it was depressingly correct.

I was a bewildered New Haven freshman when "Bill's book" fell upon a startled campus and exploded it into controversy. Indeed, I had hardly had time to become acquainted with the world of Yale before I found myself confronted with, and partially engaged in, a furious dialogue on its virtues and demerits.

The dispute which unfolded around *God and Man* was an education in itself. The Yale of 1951 was a community in which Liberalism, among faculty and undergraduates alike, ruled virtually without challenge. I had begun to sense this fact on my own, but the response to Bill's book vastly accelerated my understanding of it. For it established that Yale's fidelity to "free inquiry" was peculiarly selective—that it did not extend to conservative inquiries about the political impact of the Yale curriculum.

God and Man consisted of two parts: first, a critique of the intellectual tendency of a Yale education, canvassing curricular and extracurricular pressures; and second, a theory of "academic freedom" designed to correct that tendency. The first was simply a matter of empirical reckoning, and it was, as of 1951, prudently conceived and accurately rendered. The second, resting on a system of value premises challenging received notions of modern education, supplied a legitimate basis for contention.

While Buckley's descriptive and analytical passages, on what I had observed, seemed to me painstakingly correct, they stirred an almost irrational anger in the rest of the Yale community. The *Yale Daily News* struck out at its former chairman with passionate detestation; the administration piously disavowed Buckley's charge of collectivist and agnostic tendencies (quite to the satisfaction of the alumni). Buckley was roundly denounced as a button-down Torquemada, an advocate of "conformity," who would suppress "dissent" on American campuses.

The irony of all this, from my point of view, was that it was Buckley who represented "dissent," and his massed critics who represented "conformity." With one exception, I cannot recall—during my freshman year—ever meeting or hearing of a Yale student or professor who rallied to Buckley's defense (I did run into a few in subsequent years). As for the world beyond the campus, the monumental lethargy of the alumni, who either could not have cared less or else hurried to defend the Yale administration, offered convincing evidence as to what was the real "conformity" in our society, and who was in fact engaged in "dissent."

A few of my own impressions, gathered at random, may serve to establish the intellectual climate of that day, and to explain my reasons for seconding Buckley's description of Yale at the turn of the half-century.

When I had got settled on the Old Campus, and turned my attention to the Yale *News,* I found its editorial page bristling with sentiments that would have done credit—to phrase the matter gently—to Americans for Democratic Action. The Chairman, John Steadman, was an able and aggressive polemicist for the left. Jim Thomson, who succeeded Steadman the second semester of that year, was of the same persuasion.

Under such guidance, the *News* adhered to an impeccable policy of Liberalism, which was not always confined to the editorial page. When I was competing to get on the staff of the paper, the "heelers," as we were called, received frequent lectures on the importance of objectivity. When dealing with controversial topics, the managing editor warned us, we should make sure personal bias did not affect our writing. Mindful of these strictures, I took occasion at one editorial meeting to protest a headline blatantly loaded against that *bête-noire* of the early fifties, Senator McCarthy. The head described McCarthy as "invading" a college campus (i.e., going to a school to deliver an address). "We have been told," I said, "to be objective in handling controversial news. It seems to me this headline prostitutes the front page to innuendo against McCarthy."

The managing editor was irate. "I am glad to prostitute my front page," he said, "if it hurts Joe McCarthy."

That statement of journalistic ethics, it seems to me, incapsulates the Liberal view which then reigned at Yale—as it did, and still does, in much of the American intellectual community. In this conception, honesty demands rigorous attention to fact, a hearing for all disputants, and no weighting of the scales against one side or the other—except, of course, when dealing with Joe McCarthy, or Bill Buckley, or some other conservative demon.

The controversial senator, needless to say, was the favorite target for ridicule, attack, and condescending allusion. He provided a convenient test of Yale's commitment to hearing "both sides" before rendering judgment—a test which faculty and undergraduates failed repeatedly, and with obvious relish.

I recall one discussion group in a religion course, in which the professor, one Burton MacLean, posed the following question: "Suppose you were a Christian in ancient Rome, and Senator McCaesar called you before his committee and asked you about your participation in this allegedly subversive group. What would you do?" A not untypical approach for a Yale professor—suggesting both the predispositions of the faculty, and the ease with which they could be injected into seemingly irrelevant subject matter.

The Yale religion department had come in for special scrutiny in *God and Man* and I found much in my one brush with it to suggest that Buckley was justified in indicting it as, at best, a feeble support for the convictions of religious students. The influence of the Yale curriculum, particularly in the social sciences, was heavily weighted toward the proposition that belief in God is irrational—a sociological phenomenon, based on primitive apprehensions of death. Far from countering this theory, the Yale religion department, in at least one instance with which I am familiar, lent it tacit support. In the religion course I took we used a textbook arguing that Judaism owed its unique emphasis on monotheism, not to revelation, but to "evolutionary" development from an earlier polytheism. This theory —which, incidentally, does not seem to be supported by the relevant biblical texts—leads the student to accept the view that the Judaeo-Christian religion is simply an anthropological construction.

In the secular realm, the influence of Yale classes and texts, when at all to the point, was usually to push the student toward acceptance of statism, or collectivism. The basic economics text was Paul Samuelson's *Economics, an Introductory Analysis*—an unblushing brief for Keynesian interventionism. The basic sociology course ended with a fervent peroration in behalf of city planning. The basic political science course included a potent lecture by the celebrated Cecil Driver, implanting in students' minds the idea that the coming of Socialism was inevitable.

Students more often than not accepted such views as authoritative comment on matters of political philosophy. There was little inclination to challenge, e.g., Professor Driver's eloquent demonstration that Western man was ordained to live under collectivism. On the contrary, when I was in the course, that particular lecture was greeted with a standing ovation by 400 students.

Such was the Yale of the early 1950's. It was a world in which a student of conservative inclination found himself badly in need of help, counsel, and information. By chance encounter, early in my sojourn at Yale, I came upon sources which were to supply all three.

Late in my freshman year I wandered into Liggett's drugstore on the corner of York and Elm. Browsing at the newsstand, I came across a magazine called *The Freeman*. From its format, the magazine looked like any of a number of "little" periodicals, and I assumed it was yet another Liberal publication. To my amazement, I found it was strongly anti-Communist, and an eloquent proponent of free market economics. It was something of a landmark—the first time I had ever laid eyes on a conservative periodical of any sort.

A second encounter followed a philosophy class, in which I had engaged in a mild colloquy with Professor Paul Weiss, on the subject of states' rights. Afterward, a student came up to me and handed me a card. It contained two notations: "Intercollegiate Society of Individualists" and "Foundation for Economic Education." "These groups think along lines like yours," he said. "You might want to get on their mailing list."

From these three organizations—*The Freeman,* ISI, and FEE—I was able to gather information useful to me in my groping attempt to weigh the significance of events, to assess the impact of course material. *The Freeman* carried a number of articles on raging national controversies—particularly the smouldering question of internal security. Through ISI, I received books by Frederic Bastiat, Frank Chodorov, and F. A. Harper—explaining the principles of the free market; the Washington newsletter, *Human Events;* and booklets from FEE. I became aware of the existence of conservative publishers—Henry Regnery and Devin-Adair. With a little effort, I found books from each at the Yale Co-op—Charles Callan Tansill's *Back Door to War,* and Frank Chodorov's *One is a Crowd.*

This literature offered welcome information—but it was more than that. From the perspective of 1961, the slight quantity of materials then available to a conservative student may not seem impressive. But to me, it was a discovery beyond price; for it meant that I was no longer alone. Here were men of reputation—scholars, journalists, publishers—who shared my uneasiness, and who brought factual support and theoretical subtlety to the conservative cause.

It was on such foundations that the semblance of a conservative movement was launched at Yale. By the time I reached my junior year, we had gathered together a little nucleus of conservative-minded students. Some of us had met at the Political Union, where we held forth as a vocal minority in "the Party of the Right." One member of that group was Gridley Wright, then a sophomore. Early in January, Grid called me and asked me to come to a meeting in his room. He had been to Whitlock's and the Co-op, he said, in search of some basic conservative books. The proprietors had never heard of them. What we needed, Grid believed, was to form a library of our own—to make conservative books available to interested students. The idea took hold, and, with the aid of the Foundation for Economic Education and ISI, the library was formed. It was the beginning of the conservative counterattack at Yale.

"The Independent Library," as it was called, did not work any magical conversion. Indeed, as a lending institution, it was something of a failure. More students came there to argue with the librarians than to read. But we were satisfied that we had at least served notice that conservatism at Yale was alive (contrary to popular report), and the Library soon became the center for a number of other activities.

In late 1954, we decided our efforts should be directed toward awakening students to the bias in some of the course material. We resolved upon a publication, in which we would conduct a critique of lectures and textbooks, to demonstrate that the canons of "academic freedom" were being only partially observed in New Haven.

This proved to be our most sensational effort, provoking criticism in the Yale *News* and a flood of hostile letters, and providing a durable topic of campus controversy. It also provoked, I am happy to recall, favorable comment from some of the faculty—notably Professor L. P. Curtis of the History Department, and Professor Eugene V. Rostow, presently dean of the Yale Law School.

The philosophy behind *The Independent*, as we called our publication, was that, as students, we were not equipped to pontificate on world and national issues. But we did consider ourselves authorities on one thing—the type of course material we were receiving in class. In consequence, we carried critiques of textbooks, such as Parrington and Rowley, and of particular courses, such as Economics 10 and Political Science 10a.

From our base at the Independent Library, our small band of ten or so conservatives attempted to work outward into the Yale community. And although we flattered ourselves that we were making progress with this or that minor victory, our over-all performance was not impressive. We tried to galvanize the Party of the Right, and staged one strong campaign to get control of the Political Union. This effort, although valiant, was rebuffed, and conservative activity in that organization sub-sided.

We also revived the Calliopean Society—a famous Yale de-bating club of the 19th century. We held several meetings the last semester of my senior year, and considered the group a smashing success. Yet it was only a ripple on the placid surface of Yale's omnipresent Liberalism. As for more direct political movements, we considered the Young Republicans at Yale some-thing of a lost cause. The YR club was authentically "modern," and it never occurred to us that it could be much of anything else. On the whole, we tried hard, and we made the community aware that conservatism was around. But we had only begun, and had few tangible achievements to show for our effort.

In February, 1960, just five years after we brought out the first issue of *The Independent,* I was invited back to Yale to speak before the Calliopean Society. And I found that things had changed. To my astonishment, Calliopean, far from lapsing into inaction as I had feared, was operating at a tempo and with an enthusiasm unheard-of in 1955. Under the leadership of a young man named David Stuhr, it was holding a meeting a week, and playing host to some of the most noted speakers in the conservative camp—Fulton Lewis, Robert Morris, William

Rusher. The membership was larger, the clamor for admission louder.*

The difference between Calliopean, 1955, and Calliopean, 1960, sums up the history of undergraduate conservatism at Yale. The Society, when I was in school, was our most successful venture. It is far more successful now. And in other fields, where our efforts were either rebuked or only partially effective, the new Yale conservatives were moving ahead at full throttle. The Young Republican club was no longer "modern" but solidly conservative (a change also characteristic of Young Republicans around the country). In the Political Union, where our effort had failed and then lapsed altogether, a rejuvenated Party of the Right had gained control. The President was—unthinkable in my day—a member of that party, and an unabashed conservative. In every aspect, the conservative movement was stronger, more resilient, more aggressive, than it was when I departed in June, 1955.

Since then, I am informed, the Yale conservatives have become even more active and more influential. Their numbers are greater, their position on campus more prestigious. The Calliopean Society, I have been happy to see, has even gained some off-campus notoriety for its activities. It begins to appear that "individualism"—or commitment to America's traditional conception of limited government—may yet survive at Yale. And if it does at last expire, it will not be without a fight.

This history of undergraduate politics offers, I believe, a paradigm of the young conservative movement throughout the country. What in 1951 had been only the inkling of disagree-

* The vigorous continuity of Calliopean is owing, in particular, to a series of energetic leaders like Stuhr, Alan Buchmann, Wayne Holman, Dean Secord, George Decas, and Jack Kahn.

ment, sensed by a few scattered individuals, and in 1953 had been merely a faltering effort to pose an alternative to the Liberal orthodoxy, has now become a full-blooded and purposeful movement. By common report, conservatism among American young people is on the upswing. The sudden volte-face of the young, indeed, has become topic A among those who watch over American campuses, and has spurred a considerable amount of speculation and controversy. No one seems quite to know what it is all about, what has caused it, or where it is going.

This book has been written to shed some light on these matters. I claim for it no conclusive insights. It is perforce limited by my own limitations—both in gathering the facts in the case and in articulating their significance—and it concerns a phenomenon which is changing rapidly from month to month. Thus the view here offered is necessarily fragmentary and impressionistic. My effort has been to suggest the general conditions which created the conservative rebellion, to describe the premises upon which it is proceeding, and to identify the principal individuals and organizations that have led the way in bringing it about. I have tried to intimate the range and potency of the movement in broad terms, and to describe the techniques and the stages by which individual efforts, such as our program at Yale, have merged into larger patterns of activity, and at last become wedded in the confluence of a national movement. In that attempt, I have necessarily omitted reference to many people who have played a part in this activity. In particular, it has been impossible to take note of all the various campus organizations, and the individuals composing them, who have contributed, and who are contributing, to this endeavor. To these my apologies are extended herewith.

Throughout this essay, I have used the words "conservative"

and "Liberal" to identify the rebels and those against whom they are rebelling. The matter of appropriate definitions for these terms is, I grant, a vexed point in contemporary politics. Yet I shall forego the usual practice of stating my own formal definitions at the outset, for a double reason. The first reason is that the Liberal-conservative terminology is now in common use in our society, and so will, I trust, provide the reader with a generally satisfactory notion of what is being described. The second is that the ideological content of Liberalism, and by inference of its conservative alternative, is the principal subject of my first chapter, which I have approached by working outward from a critique of our troubled society. My own definitions of Liberalism and conservatism, with their reversed conceptions of value and human freedom, fall logically after this discussion, rather than before it.

M.S.E.
Indianapolis, Indiana
June, 1961

I

The New Conformity

"Only connect. . . ."

E. M. FORSTER

IF WE MAY BELIEVE what we read, the United States today is a nation oppressed by conformity. Professional critics of our society have discovered that we are suffering from a form of intellectual and moral paralysis. Where once we had been a land of self-reliant pioneers, we are told, we have become a land of groups and aggregates. We are increasingly afraid to think and act for ourselves; a degenerate citizenry prefers the comforts of "belongingness" and "togetherness" to the splendid rigors of independence.

Such commentary, at least in its more fashionable variations, is generally limited to surface matters. The nation is asked to do penance for its commuter mores and split-level ethics, but is given neither an alternative to the mores, nor a reason for the penance. Criticism of this sort is represented, most famously, by Professor John Kenneth Galbraith, of Cambridge and New Delhi, and by a journalist named Vance Packard. Packard has been particularly voluble—producing three somber elegies for our vanished individualism, toiling through endless volumes of sociological data, piling fact upon fact, demonstrating that we are a nation of juiceless automatons.

Messrs. Packard and Galbraith are but two of a melancholy chorus summoning us to retribution, proclaiming the default of individual initiative, the erosion of excellence beneath the pressures of the mass. They conclude, in Professor Galbraith's words, that we have become a nation in which "the bland lead the bland."

Such criticisms may have a tonic effect if they alert us, as I believe they do, to some authentic failing. But their own failure is that they tell us little or nothing about the *causes* of our difficulty, the social processes which have reduced us to our conformist estate. To determine that, it is necessary to see the paraphernalia of "belongingness," not as incidental phenomena, but as part of a systemic disorder in the heart of society and the soul of man. And this far the Packards and the Galbraiths will not go.

Other critics have approached the matter with greater discernment, if with similar hesitation. These are men disenchanted with the going order, but apparently cherishing emotional commitments to it too strong to relinquish. I have in mind such humane students of the age as David Riesman, Lionel Trilling, Jacques Barzun—men of complex sensitivity and discriminating mind. Respected members of the academic community, they have created a small genre of criticism aimed at keeping that community faithful to the canons of excellence, and of freedom.

Perhaps the most enlightening of this school is David Riesman, the Harvard sociologist, who has systematically probed the tissue of our society, and found it diseased. Riesman's habit is to work with sociological studies, as does Packard, but to shape them into significant patterns, rather than stringing them endlessly together. His concern is to describe our condition, but more importantly to discover the causes of it. In that effort, he has produced several books relevant to the present inquiry, the most notable of which is entitled *The Lonely Crowd.* This work, a belletristic rendering of sociological data, documents the disappearance of individualism from our national life, and creates a terminology which I shall venture to use in this discussion. The classic American, in Riesman's categories, was "inner-directed"—meaning he was self-reliant and individualistic, guiding his thought and behavior by an internalized system of values. The new species, the inhabitant of the lonely crowd, is "other-directed"—meaning he cues his behavior and his ideas to the group. It adds up to "an enormous ideological shift favoring submission to the group, a shift whose decisiveness is concealed by the persistence of older ideological patterns."

The apprehensions of the disenchanted, and the particular findings of Riesman's survey, have been amplified by William H. Whyte, an editor of *Fortune.* In his book called *The Organization Man* Whyte describes America as heading for an environment in which "everyone is tightly knit into a belongingness with one another; one in which there is no restless wandering but rather the deep emotional security that comes from total integration with the group."

Riesman and Whyte, unlike Packard and Galbraith, have carried the analysis a step further, though not to the end of the reckoning. They agree that our tendency toward submersion in the group, and toward reliance on the state, stems from an alteration in fundamental values. Whereas Americans once premised their actions upon a code of morality, that code is no longer respected. And people who have no internal value system must turn elsewhere for guidance. We have seen, Whyte said, the decline of "the Protestant Ethic," which placed a premium on hard work and individual responsibility; in its place, we have adopted a variety of determinism, which places a premium on adjustment to shifting conditions, rather than on fidelity to personal values. The ideology of the mass requires, first and foremost, a surrender of moral autonomy.

Riesman found that the "inner-directed" American "is very considerably bound by traditions; they limit his ends and inhibit his means." Those traditions embody a moral code "implanted early in life . . . and directed toward generalized but nonetheless inescapably destined goals." The "other-directed" American has no such internal guidance system. "What is common to all the other-directed people is that their contemporaries are the source of direction for the individual." The "other-directed" conformist, trying to line up his own behavior with attitudes acceptable to the community, is thus always alert to find out what is *au courant* and what is not. The old-style American was a "moralizer"; the new-style is an "inside-dopester."

These are, I think, significant findings; properly construed, they can tell us a great deal about what is wrong with American society today. In particular, they grasp the essential point without which our present difficulties cannot be understood; that we are at once *permissive* in matters of ethics, *statist* in matters of public policy; that we have become the second because we became the first; and that the two feed upon one another in baleful symbiosis. And yet they are not primarily important for what they say, either because it is new—which it isn't, or because it is true—which it is. The Whyte-Riesman analysis is important because, in speaking to our society concerning its most cherished shortcomings, it is *accepted*.

And this was no small achievement. For previous efforts in this direction had met with reprisals or disdain. Warnings about the collectivization of society were of course dismissed out of hand when they came from businessmen or others presumed to have greedy reasons for favoring "rugged individualism." But things were equally unpleasant for members of the intellectual community who glimpsed the dangers of the mass, and evangelized against them. John Dos Passos and Max Eastman, to name only two, suddenly found critical and academic doors closed to them when they became uneasy about the growth of the Leviathan state. For writing that "there are no longer protagonists; there is only a chorus" (this in 1932), Jose Ortega y Gasset was pigeonholed as a quaint and irascible Cassandra; the rest of the intellectual community proceeded to harass and destroy those protagonists still left on stage. In 1950, when Riesman wrote *The Lonely Crowd,* author-editor Frank Chodorov declared that the most striking development of the half-century "was the transmutation of the American character from individualist to collectivist." The difference was that Chodorov had been saying just that for years, as had his mentor, Albert Jay Nock. And for the saying, neither Nock nor Chodorov could receive the time of day from important publishers or major journals of opinion.

The Whyte and Riesman books, in contrast, were not only accepted by important publishers; they became critical and popular triumphs. That is a fact which can hardly be overestimated. For it signifies that a society of conformists had, from various discomforts it had inflicted upon itself, at last decided to listen. A nation of "other-directed" citizens was prepared to be told it was precisely that.

I do not mean to overstress the readiness which the Whyte-Riesman breakthrough illustrated. Their acceptance was in part owing to the terms in which they couched their findings. Addressing an errant society is something like addressing an errant king. One does not convince by frontal assault; the job must be done by degrees, by making a suggestion here and a distinction there, and by mantling the whole in the semblance of consent and approbation. Thus both Whyte and Riesman, while severely critical, took pains to insure that they were not totally at odds with their community. Each was mightily concerned—as in their parallel discussions of progressive education—to make sure that he was not identified as a "reactionary" enemy of "progressivism" per se, even though it was progressivism he attacked. (That sort of diagnosis, given the new plateau of understanding, would follow in due course, but from other sources.) Their discussions, Riesman's in particular, suggest that even as they discern the imprisoning forces of the age, they are themselves imprisoned. This school sees everything that is wrong, but is apparently too conditioned by the conformity it describes to conceive of any way of getting out of it.*

This absence of fundamental counsel stirred no end of confusion among government committees and popular journalists, who in the natural order of things were at length moved to emulate the Riesmans, the Trillings, the Barzuns, and the Whytes. The mass media blossomed with dissertations on the declining American character; *Life* magazine conducted a ponderous series on the "national purpose." Alarmed by the critique of the declining national character, everyone agreed that *something* ought to be done.

And where did these analyses come out? Decrying our loss of national vigor, the seekers of goals and purposes exhibited no

---

* See, e.g., Riesman's "Values in Context," in *Individualism Reconsidered,* and the denouement of Lionel Trilling's novel, *The Middle of the Journey.* Each attempts to reject the errors of other-direction without rejecting the essence of it or embracing its alternative.

notion of what had caused it. Indeed, their recommendations for a cure were usually for more of the same.

From the matter just reviewed, it appears that dependence on the state, or on the collectivity, is intimately related to the decline of the American character. Yet the net conclusion of the "national purpose" series was that we could rebuild that character by cracking down on "privatism," concentrating more on the common good. President Eisenhower's commission on goals, declaring its fealty to individual self-reliance, suggested that several billion dollars be added to the federal budget for handouts. Professor Galbraith, anointing himself as a truculent iconoclast, suggests we can escape "blandness" by taking money away from private citizens, and letting the government spend it instead. Point counterpoint—even unto the White House itself, where we find President Kennedy one day urging his countrymen to struggle and sacrifice, the next inviting them to batten upon the federal Treasury.

In such a welter of confusion, it is hardly surprising that the critics of "conformity" have had a hard time scaring up a young folks' rebellion against it. And a rebellion, of course, there had to be. A nation of sclerotic tendency has a right to expect its young people to do something about it. And so the search began. Looking under every bush, the secondary oracles came up with some unlikely specimens. Writing in *The Nation*, Kenneth Rexroth professed to see a surge of youthful rebellion in "peace and disarmament meetings." Several newspapers opined that students who reviled the House Un-American Activities Committee were the "new wave." *Look* magazine chimed in with a tribute to the "explosive generation." "Conformity," it allowed, was getting its come-uppance in the sit-in demonstrations in the South. Murray Kempton

wrapped them all up in *The Progressive,* claiming that the *real*
rebellion of our times "shows itself in demonstrations against
the Un-American Activities Committee or in marches for a
nuclear ban or in sit-downs against Southern segregation laws."

But none of this would quite do. Whatever personal hazards
young people may have experienced in such enterprises, there
was certainly nothing rebellious, in a serious philosophical
sense, about the opinions they professed. Opposition to nuclear
testing, after all, has for some years been the official stance of
the United States government; animosity toward the House
Un-American Activities Committee bears the considerable ca-
chet of *The New York Times* and other pillars of the journalistic community; and the campaign against Southern segregation
is in the nature of a transpartisan national vendetta. Indeed, if
we examine the constituent elements of our "conformity"
closely, we shall find that aggravated pacifism, elastic "tolerance" of Communists, and militant egalitarianism are all extensions of the prevailing ethic. The students' gestures, however exaggerated, were simply a case of *plus ça se révolte, plus
c'est la même chose.*

So too with the most publicized stand-in for youthful rebellion, the "beat generation." The beats, in one way or another,
have become involved in all of the movements mentioned
above, although it is safe to say that for the most part they are
profoundly indifferent to such matters. The average beatnik
certainly fits the conventional description of a "rebel." He rejects the visible icons of the new conformity—ranchwagons and
the comforts of suburbia. But because he has been given no
reliable analysis of what has *created* this pall of sameness, his
impulse to rebellion is mischanneled and ultimately thwarted.
For the common philosophy of the beats—the rejection of value,
the submersion in subjective apprehension—is in fact the pre-

vailing philosophy of the age. The root affirmations of beat nihilism are also the root affirmations of positivism and pragmatism, which have, in their popular modulations, presided over our descent into the mass. Philosophically, it would be hard to slip a piece of paper between the beat nihilist and Riesman's other-directed man. Both are fugitives from value.

When the critics had thus examined every by-way in bohemia, and found nothing very substantial, they gave it up as a bad job. Young people today, they concluded, are hopeless. Some called them "the silent generation." Others indicted them for timidity. In seeking "rebellion," the searchers instead had found, to their horror, a growing "conservatism." In the Washington *Post* columnist Malvina Lindsay clucked over the emergence of "the young fogies," who tended to adopt a conservative stance on political issues. The Louisville *Courier-Journal* brooded: "There was a time when the college years were years of intellectual ground-breaking, of ferment, of impassioned commitment to new ideas. . . . But, alas, this is no longer the case. Survey after survey detects a growing conservatism and conformity and fear of controversy on the college campus."

Such observations bespeak the same confusion which sends *Life* magazine in search of the national character, and brings it home lambasting "privatism." The seekers of youthful rebellion set out upon their quest without knowing what the Grail looked like. They had not troubled to define "conformity," and so had no conception of authentic rebellion. Instead, they accepted the procedural stereotype—itself common to the conformist mind—which holds that "rebellion" is always and necessarily a function of the political left, on the analogy of the radical son rejecting the values of his conservative father. They sought rebellion with the eyes of orthodoxy, and they could find nothing.

The confusion might have been avoided if Whyte and Riesman had pressed their criticisms on to the end, or even if the
secondary oracles had troubled to study the Whyte-Riesman
analysis for the lessons implicit in it. For what was needed, obviously, was some substantive determination as to the nature
and sources of the conformity. Only with that established can
we define the necessary shape of rebellion; without it, we shall
start repeatedly at random bursts of excitement, looking to each
as the impulse which will liberate us from sameness—and we
shall be forever disappointed.

I have briefly reviewed the findings of Whyte, Riesman, and
the other critics of our conformity. Let me elaborate upon them
a bit further, to arrive at more certain understanding of our
difficulties.

Permissiveness. As a nation, we have lost our attachment to
the values of "the Protestant Ethic." We no longer believe in
the absolute standards of behavior handed down by our tradition. We have become determinists, pragmatists, trimmers. We
are no longer concerned with doing what is "right" but with
"getting along," adjusting.

As a result of our declining values, we tend, derivatively, to
adopt a spurious "tolerance" towards matters which in a former day would have been considered wrong. We are losing our
moral sense.

Statism. We have tended to yield the governance of our lives
to the group, or to the state. We no longer believe in individual
self-reliance, but prefer to huddle in the shadow of the mass.

In the urge to "adjust," to achieve group harmony, we have
abandoned our notions of personal and technical excellence;
we are rapidly reducing our society to the lowest common denominator of intelligence and skill.

Such are the components of modern conformity. It remains

simply to say, in the context of modern society, what that conformity most closely resembles. And is there any student of our politics who cannot identify the ideas sketched above?

At the level of value, what philosophy is it that tells us there are no fixed standards of performance? That preaches that all things are relative, and that we can never know right from wrong? What philosophy tells us that individuals are not free agents, but puppets driven by economic circumstance? That, e.g., a juvenile delinquent—particularly one from a broken or a penurious home—is not to blame for his behavior?

In public policy, what philosophy has preached that "rugged individualism" is at best obsolete, at worst an unmitigated evil? That we must consider the claims of society above those of the individual? That we must have compulsory alms for farmers, businessmen, the unemployed, and even entire cities?

What philosophy tells us that there is but one absolute in our society, the will of the majority? That "democracy," meaning the will of 51% of a given constituency, must at all costs prevail? That our schools should be conducted for the benefit of, and at a pace congenial to, the most retarded?

The matter, I think, is clear enough. The conformity of our day, down to the last particular, is nothing other than the aggregate of beliefs known as "Liberalism." Indeed, its constituent elements—permissiveness in ethics, statism in politics—may be taken as the very definition of contemporary Liberal philosophy, and they are so considered throughout this discussion. Thus the earnest seekers for youthful "rebellion" could, of course, find nothing of the sort along the purlieus of the left. There they would discover merely extensions of the permissive ethics, dirigist economics, and democratist politics which are the very essence of our conformity.

Nowhere is the search for a leftward rebellion more futile

than on the college campus. For the Liberal pressures within the academy are even more intense than they are in society at large. The professoriate, by any assessment, is overwhelmingly Liberal. In a study called *The Academic Mind,* sociologists Paul Lazarsfeld and Wagner Thielens surveyed more than 2,400 college professors, and found that upwards of seventy per cent of them could be classified as Liberals. When asked whether they considered themselves "more Liberal or more conservative" than their colleagues, thirty-nine per cent said more Liberal, and only twelve per cent said more conservative. "One would logically expect," the authors say, "that on the average an equal number of teachers would consider themselves more Liberal and more conservative. Yet the self-designation of 'more Liberal' occurs over three times more often. Obviously, being politically progressive is at a premium in this sector of the professoriate."

"I happen to prefer champagne to dishwater," said Justice Oliver Wendell Holmes, "but there is no reason to suppose the cosmos does." That permissive epigram is the motto of the American academy, as well as the epitaph of the Western mind. Various attitude tests show that college professors tend to be relativists, agnostics, or atheists far more frequently than the rest of us. And their attitudes are effectively imparted to their students. "Living in this kind of atmosphere," wrote a Catholic student at Princeton, "is hardly conducive to strengthening one's religion. Mine has taken a terrible beating."

Matters are no better with regard to statism, which the average faculty member tends to accept without much hesitation. As a student publication at the University of Wisconsin observes, "the curriculum is replete with justifications of government-centered economic action." One informed observer believes no less than ninety per cent of the economics professors in the

United States are followers of Lord Keynes, teaching that the government must manipulate the economy to insure "full employment." The estimate is fully supported by the fact that Samuelson's *Economics, an Introductory Analysis,* is the nation's most widely used economics textbook. At last count, it was being employed in no less than 515 American colleges, while a non-Keynesian work of equal competence, Van Sickle and Rogge's *Introduction to Economics,* was being used in less than half-a-dozen.

Keynesian economics teaches the student he must consider economic activity, not from the perspective of the individual, but from the perspective of the "national income." He must think not in terms of incentives and opportunities, but in terms of vast aggregates, which the government is enjoined to manipulate. As a student at Yale put it, in 1957:

In our instruction we were led to believe that economic forces can and should be controlled by Government. One textbook, Adams' *Structure of American Industry,* advocated that some federal action be taken with respect to almost every industry. One whole section of our course was devoted to Socialism; we were required to read only two conservative articles during the year. We were told that the gold standard was an evil, that the income tax should be of a strongly progressive nature, and that the only reason the New Deal failed in eliminating the Depression was that its policies were not carried far enough.

Such ideas can be found throughout the curriculum. In a study of commonly used textbooks in sociology, A. H. Hobbs of the University of Pennsylvania concluded: "Emphasis in sociology texts is markedly critical of private competitive enterprise and of capitalistic economy."

The preference for "groupism" has been effectively transmitted to the majority of the student population. In a survey

called *Changing Values in College,* Professor Philip E. Jacob
finds that today's college students are the very image of Riesman's "other-directed" man: "Students cheerfully expect to
conform to the economic status quo and to receive ample re-
wards for dutiful and productive effort. American students are
likewise dutifully responsive toward government. They expect
to obey its laws, pay its taxes, serve in its armed forces—without
complaint but without enthusiasm."

That the students' attitudes come from the teaching they receive can hardly be doubted. A survey in the Harvard *Crimson*
reveals that "lectures and assigned readings" had influenced
a huge segment of the undergraduate body to become more
Liberal—*i.e.,* more favorably disposed toward government manipulation of individual lives.

Sometimes these facts are subject to angry denial—as when
Bill Buckley alleged them against Yale. But on occasion, an
exultant Liberal cannot help but survey the triumph of permissive-statist pedagogy, and confirm the obvious. Thus Joseph
Clark, now a Democratic Senator from Pennsylvania, some
years ago rejoiced that "Adlai Stevenson has more supporters
among the school-teachers and college professors than Tom
Dewey." And, Clark added, "It is significant that what used to
be called 'history' is now 'social studies.' *Spiritually and eco-
nomically youth is conditioned to respond to a Liberal program
of orderly policing of our society by government, subject to the
popular will, in the interests of social justice.*" (Italics added.)

In view of that disarming confession, is it any mystery that
our society has been propelled away from individual self-
reliance, and toward submission to the group? And is it any
mystery that the search for youthful rebellion in the ranks of
Liberaldom issued in a failure? Our Liberal academicians have
worked diligently for thirty years to extinguish America's faith

in the individual, and then they express amazement that we have lost our self-reliance! "We make men without chests," C. S. Lewis observed, "and expect of them virtue and enterprise. We laugh at honour and are shocked to find traitors in our midst. We castrate and bid the geldings be fruitful."

Clearly, the conformity afflicting American society and the American campus is Liberalism. And the signs of conservatism, glimpsed so unhappily by Malvina Lindsay and the Louisville *Courier-Journal,* were the beginning of insurrection.

II

The Shape of Rebellion

"... Laskell saw that the intellectual power had gone from that system of idealism, and much of its power of drama had gone. The time was getting ripe for a competing system. And it would be brought by the swing of the pendulum, not by the motion of growth."

LIONEL TRILLING

IT WAS, FOR AMERICAN LIBERALISM, the worst of times. The decade had begun well enough. A magistrate committed to Liberal doctrine, certified by Americans for Democratic Action, had assumed the leadership of the nation. The faculty of Harvard University had migrated, en bloc, to Washington. Programs, reports, studies, and manifestoes radiated in all directions. There had been nothing quite like it since 1933, and it was, we may be sure, immensely satisfying.

But the hour of achievement was haunted by misgivings. For deep within itself, America was changing. In the realm of ideas, where our politics are ultimately fashioned, Liberalism had ceased to advance, indeed seemed even to retreat. As the Kennedy administration attempted to reprise the New Deal, it became clear that Liberal doctrine had little to offer that was new. More sensitive members of the Liberal community had long since turned introspective and disconsolate. The nation as a whole was uncertain, grasping for principle and resolution. Worst of all, an ideological counterattack was under way. From the loins of introspection and misgiving, there had sprung a literature of dissent. The findings of the Riesmans and the Whytes could not be unsaid, and they were daily supplemented by even more emphatic repudiations of the statist ethic.

So it happened that, in its hour of triumph, Liberalism felt the earth begin to shift beneath its feet. The element upon which it had lavished its most fervent hopes, the very element supposedly symbolized by the exuberant clan of Kennedys ("We're a young group," Attorney General-to-be Robert Kennedy had said the preceding summer, "and we're taking over"), had somehow, unpredictably, bolted off in the wrong direction. The nation's youth, everyone discovered at once, was turning conservative. Instead of asking for *more* government interference in their lives, American young people wanted less; instead of "accommodations" with the Communists, they wanted firmness; instead of "abolishing" our internal security program, they wanted it strengthened; instead of flux and impermanence, they wanted value, tradition, the predicates of freedom and the norms of honor.

If there is a single publication by which we may gauge the tendency of the times, it must surely be *The New Yorker*. No other journal so elegantly combines the comforts of privilege with the glamor of dissent—that admixture of chic and iconoclasm which in our society marks the received, the anointed, and the superbly upper-middle-class. It was thus a matter of some importance to find, in an issue of that magazine, a drawing of two gentlemen at cocktails in the Stygian comfort of their Club. One of them saying: "Then we have another son—a radical—who's joined Barry Goldwater's conservatives."

There is other symbolic matter. I recall a New York television show some months ago, a panel discussion on the political temper of American youth. The participants were Max Lerner, a venerable though still pugnacious Liberal; Douglas Caddy, an official of a conservative youth group called Young Americans for Freedom; and William A. Rusher, the youthful publisher of the conservative magazine, *National Review*. What the panelists said added up to the fact that there was a conservative revival among the young; but their identities, and their appearance, said it even more eloquently. Lerner, his leathery visage reflecting years of combat in the lists; and on either side of him the bright, unlined faces of youth, engaged in passionate advocacy of conservatism. I could not help feeling a twinge of empathy. What must Lerner have been thinking, as he grappled with these contumacious youngsters? How could he fit this strange encounter into his catalogue of Liberal imperatives? Whatever his thoughts, he was the image of the faltering Old Guardsman, perplexed and discomfited by heretical novelties.

Such episodes suggest the paradox of the age. For it is indeed the Liberal who is old—who has aged in the comfortable exercise of power—and it is the conservative who is young, angry, declassé. The evidence of conservative rebellion—substantive as well as symbolic—is everywhere at hand.

In Washington, D.C., a group of young conservative pickets, demonstrating in favor of the House Un-American Activities Committee, outnumber leftists parading against the committee; conservative youth organizations, with names like "Intercollegiate Society of Individualists" and "Young Americans for Freedom" number memberships in the thousands; at Villanova, the Student Council votes, 38 to 11, in favor of retaining the loyalty provisions in the National Defense Education Act; a squadron of young Republican Congressmen, elected in 1960, declare themselves "Goldwater Republicans"; in New York, a rally of conservative youth jams Manhattan Center, and turns away thousands; at Michigan State, the campus conservative club receives a national award for its patriotic ardor, and stages a rally for Senator Barry Goldwater that is attended by 3500 people; at college book stores across the nation, Goldwater's book, *The Conscience of a Conservative,* is the number-one best seller.

The phenomenon which had annoyed Malvina Lindsay and depressed the Louisville *Courier* simply would not down. Instead, with each passing month, it grew more obstreperous, more embarrassing and more impossible to ignore. Slowly and by degrees, the story made its way to the public. Publications like *National Review* and *Human Events* had been calling attention to it for some months. Then the *Wall Street Journal* and *Time* magazine discovered what was happening; *Newsweek* took note, as did the Scripps-Howard chain, and the *Chicago Tribune;* newspapers like the *Richmond Times-Dispatch,* the *Houston Chronicle,* the *Los Angeles Times* all had a look. The journals of the left tagged after, grumbling. "Sophomoric" said *Commonweal;* "futile" said the *Progressive:* "scurrilous" said *The National Guardian.* And the *Worker* thought it meant war.

To understand the cause of all this concern, one needs merely to wander on to a college campus. More likely than not, his eye will fall upon a flyer, or a sign, or a newspaper notice, announcing the next meeting of the local conservative club. He is also apt to find, in the pages of the school paper, a report on some raging controversy between Liberals and conservatives—concerning the House Un-American Activities Committee, nuclear testing, the National Student Association or any one of a dozen other such topics. The rise of the conservative clubs has rejuvenated political thinking on college campuses, enlivened once

flaccid discussions of issues, and produced the first wave of independent thinking in the schools since the 1930s.

Examples of conservative revival are virtually endless. At
Antioch College, long a citadel of extreme Liberalism, young
conservatives J. David Coldren and Frank Resnik preside over
a thriving "Conservative Forum"; at Yale, the "Party of the
Right" has become the most active party in the Political Union;
in Cambridge, conservatives have assumed the presidency of
the Student Council and of the International Relations Council; at the State University of Iowa, a young lady named Sarah
Slavin has led a surge of conservative activity; at the University
of Wisconsin, young conservatives dominate campus discussion; at Williams in Massachusetts and Queens College in New
York, there are active organizations known as the "Young Conservatives." At Tulane there is a magazine called *Liberator*—
which features articles by national figures like Barry Goldwater,
interviews with conservative intellectuals like Frank S. Meyer.
At the University of Richmond, there has sprung up a "University Forum on Conservative Government."

There are conservative clubs almost everywhere one looks;
William and Mary, Rutgers, Minnesota, Rollins, Washington,
Maryland, USC, Holy Cross, Rosary, Detroit, Iowa, Wabash,
Kansas, Indiana, Miami. They have been springing up so rapidly that in the next Congress any school without one may be
qualified to apply for assistance as a depressed area. The movement has even extended to the secondary school level. Early in
1961, for example, a student named Robert Edwards launched
a conservative club at the New York Military Academy. In
Shreveport, Louisiana, high school pupil Tommie Welch has
established a chapter of Young Americans for Freedom. At
Shortridge High School in Indianapolis there is a "Conserva-

tive Students Association," launched by a young man named Janis Starcs.

The movement has supplied the press with some elegant and unusual names. At Yale, the conservative group is known as the Calliopean Society; at Harvard, the Athenaeum*; at Princeton, the Cliosophic Party; at the University of Pennsylvania, the Eleutherian Society; at Purdue, the Society for Individual Insight; at Pitt, the Society for Conservative Studies; at Stanford, the Western Society. And the Cornell Conservative Club sponsors a magazine entitled, with antique grandiloquence, *The Gentlemen of the Right*—one of some ten or a dozen journals published by young conservatives.

Somehow, it has struck everyone as a stunning surprise—a turn of events unheard-of in American politics. But it should have been no surprise at all. For not only did the prevalence of Liberal orthodoxy suggest the likelihood of a conservative rebellion; signs of the conservative demarche had repeatedly appeared before. But, in the manner of such overtures, they were variously misconstrued or ignored until the movement they foretold was almost full-grown.

A youthful swing toward conservatism came immediately after World War II—most of it channeled into direct political action. The famous "class of '46"—the group of conservative Republicans swept into the first post-war Congress—was a beneficiary and an expression of this trend. But the momentum of that effort was dissipated, in the opinion of some of those close to it, by its overcommitment to the Republican Party. "We were conservatives, all right," says one of the participants, "but we thought political action was the answer to everything. We

* Lately superseded, I am informed, by other conservative groups in Cambridge.

became so totally involved with the Republicans that, when the party started drifting left, we went along. Our conservative instincts were muffled in the 'modernism' of the GOP."

A second surge toward the right occurred some four to five years later, propelled by a group called Students For America. SFA was intensely nationalistic, and proffered a broad, unsophisticated appeal for renascent "Americanism." But the times, and SFA's approach, were apparently not right. The movement did not survive, although a number of the students active in it continued to work in behalf of conservative principle, and have played influential roles in the current revival.

A special symptom of youthful rebellion, mentioned previously, was the "beat generation." The beat protest has been interpreted as a leftward movement, and indeed many of the beats have become involved, somewhat haphazardly, in leftist enterprises, and have carried the permissiveness of modern conformity to its *reductio ad absurdum*. But although the beats have not grasped the connection between ethical relativism and the rise of "togetherness," they at least made it clear that togetherness was not their cup of tea. The world against which the beatnik reacts is not the world of conservatism, with its emphasis on volition and variety, but of Liberalism, with its insistence upon external uniformity. Those astounded by the conservative rebellion should consider the beat hero commemorated by Jack Kerouac, whose "chief hate was Washington bureaucracy; second to that, Liberals; then cops," and who would sit for hours and execrate the compulsory pretensions of labor unions.

Thus there were at least three bursts of rebellion, in the post-war decade, against the Liberal orthodoxy: one funneled into the Republican Party, one into a premature effort at a new national organization, and one into the exotic recesses of bohemia. None did the job; but each signified a growing dis-satisfaction, among American youth, with the conformity of Liberalism.

Meanwhile, there were tentative efforts at conservative action on a number of campuses: at Yale, at Harvard, at Queens College in New York. Each of these, in its way, flourished for a year or so, and then subsided. The oracles of our society were none the wiser. But it ought to have been clear that things would not end there. These were the preliminary sounds of thunder which, though they fade momentarily, herald the advancing storm.

By late 1960, the storm had arrived. Suddenly, presidential polls on American campuses showed students inclining heavily toward the Republicans. In the Big Ten, Vice President Nixon often achieved majorities of two-to-one over Senator Kennedy. Even in Michigan, a pro-Kennedy state, Nixon carried the votes of the collegians. In Virginia, Nixon carried almost all the campus polls, compiling a majority of 259-86 at Hampden-Sydney. Faculty members, said the Richmond *Times-Dispatch,* were "surprised."

From that time forward, everyone began to pay more attention to the conservative element on campus. And by the day President Kennedy assumed office in early 1961, the awful realization had dawned. A conservative revolution was at hand.

Some Liberal commentators, at last recognizing its existence, have attempted to discount the young conservative movement. It is not, they maintain, a strong movement, nor will it be a lasting one. They assert that the appearance of a conservative revival has been created because students of *all* persuasions are more active and aggressive than hitherto. Numerically, these critics point out, conservatives form only a small minority of the student population as a whole.

On my observation, this criticism—though based on original findings which are sound enough—is untrue. It misconstrues the nature of rebellion in general, and of this one in particular.

To begin with, it does not seem to be the case that all forms of political activity among young people have been stepped up. Certainly there are active radical groups on the campus now; but five or ten years ago, the radicals were even more active, and the conservatives were almost completely silent. The only significant change has been on the conservative side of things.

The point about numbers has more validity, in the the *numerical* strength of the young conservative movement is not so great as its impact on the public consciousness might suggest. But to argue that conservatism is on the move on college campuses is not to say that all students, or even a majority of them, are conservatives. The vast majority of college students are probably neither "Liberal" nor "conservative" in the sense of holding deeply-conceived opinions on matters of political philosophy; the bulk of them might be called "Liberals," because the authorities available to them—the faculty, the textbooks, and the mass media—are Liberal. They are themselves part of the conformity.

The suggestions of a *mass* shift to conservatism, premised upon such data as Nixon's straw-vote majorities, are therefore in error. The student defection from the Democrats signifies, rather than an across-the-board change in ideology, an altered tone and mood. The factors which have caused some students to embrace conservatism, diluted to the level of unparticularized misgivings about "too much spending," have contributed to this mass phenomenon. More importantly, the special potency of the conservative revival itself has helped push the other-directed majority several steps to the right. And it is this ability to act upon and move the mass which makes the conservative movement formidable.

Rebellion against an established orthodoxy takes individual initiative, and a fair amount of courage. Possessing those qualities, the rebel tends to have certain attributes of leadership—which is the crucial point about the conservative uprising. The movement comprehends the aggressive, resourceful, and articulate members of the college community. And, as William H. Whyte puts it: "It is possible that the majority group might be less significant than the minority—that is to say, the more venturesome may become the dominant members of our society by virtue of their very disinclination to the group way."

Many young conservatives, in spite of Liberal opposition, have achieved positions of responsibility on campus newspapers, in student government, in other extracurricular endeavors. At Harvard, Howard Phillips, past President of the Student Council, and Richard Derham, 1961 Chairman of the Harvard-Radcliffe International Relations Council, are both unabashed conservatives—in spite of the fact that the student body as a whole is Liberal. At the University of Pittsburgh, conservative leader Harry W. "Woody" Turner held a variety of campus offices, and was voted "Mr. Pitt" of 1961. At Yale, conservative Michael Uhlmann is Vice Chairman of the *Daily News;* at Princeton, the principal conservative agitator, James B. Burnham, has been a featured columnist on the *Princetonian;* at Molloy College on Long Island, Annette Courtemanche, another young conservative leader, was the 1960-61 President of the Student Government; at Northwestern, Kay Wonderlic, who served as Vice-President of the Student Senate, is an outspoken conservative; Bill Dalgetty, last year's President of the Iowa student body, has been a vehement critic of the Liberal National Student Association; Dick Noble of Stanford and Scott

Stanley of Kansas are champion debaters. And so it goes.

These young people are quick to join battle in political controversies. At the University of Wisconsin, the Conservative Club, with characteristic *elan,* established a "McCarthy-Evjue" lecture series, dedicated to vindicating the late Senator Joseph R. McCarthy, and to tweaking the nose of his bitterest enemy, Madison newspaper publisher William Evjue. At Pitt, Woody Turner tackled the school administration head-on in denouncing Nikita Khrushchev's visit to the campus. A great many of these students are quite capable of holding their own with their professors, and often prove to be competent writers and gifted speakers. As I try to point out elsewhere, the young conservative movement is noteworthy for the number of talented writers it has produced, as well as for campus politicians and leaders in extracurricular activities.

These are not sponges absorbing ideological juices around them; they are opinion-makers—the people who in ten, fifteen, and twenty-five years will begin to assume the positions of power in America. They are precisely that element Arnold Toynbee calls "the creative minority." Brian Whalen of Loyola, President of the College Young Republicans of Illinois, notes the ambition of the young conservatives to obtain positions of leverage in society: "I believe students are interested in going into politics, newspaper work, and radio and television. I see the same kind of thirst for victory which has made the Liberals so outstandingly successful."*

* In support of Whalen's observation, it is worth mentioning that two former members of the conservative movement at Yale, Richard Arnold and Lewis K. Uhler, have recently moved into positions of considerable influence—as law clerk to a Supreme Court Justice, and Administrative Assistant to a United States Congressman, respectively. Other young conservatives performing important roles in government include Robert Bauman, an assistant to the House Minority Leader. In state legislatures, we find young leaders such as W. W. Hill, Jr., thirty-four, who in 1961 served as ranking member of the Ways and

As the young conservatives slake that thirst, we shall find, I think, that the student majority will continue its drift toward conservatism. For the people who simply reflect the word of "authority," and who reflect Liberal authority now, will just as easily reflect conservative authority in the years ahead.

What has spurred the students to rebel? And what do they think they are going to achieve? In talking with them, reading their literature and their various manifestoes of purpose, one gathers that, first and foremost, they are enacting the time-honored rites of youth, kicking up their heels against the reigning conformity. As *Life* observed, they are fed up with the "dull orthodox Liberalism of the academic scene." Contrasts between the attitudes of the faculty on the one hand, the students on the other, abound on most campuses. At Princeton, where the famous Clio Party recently converted itself into a full-fledged conservative club, one observer estimates the temper of the student body as anywhere from sixty to seventy per cent conservative. Reverse the statistics, he says, and you have an index to the Liberalism of the faculty.

Almost everyone who has participated in the movement confesses a strong reaction to the prevailing attitudes of the faculty. Dr. Daniel K. Stewart, himself a faculty member at Michigan State and sponsor of the MSU Conservative Club, says: "As incredible as it may seem, we see teachers telling our children that they (the teachers) are socialists, don't believe in God, don't believe in loyalty oaths . . . telling our children that they (the children) have a moral obligation to write off their parents."

Means Committee of the Indiana House. In radio and television, conservatives like Steve Slepin of Miami and Don Grider of Indianapolis are making names for themselves. Other young conservative "influentials," in intellectual activity and in politics, are discussed in Chapters VII and IX.

By some law of political oscillation, young people tend to rebel against the going order—or at least the more aggressive and resourceful young people do. Whereas the "followers" on the campus may simply repeat what is given them by their professors, those who like to speculate on problems of man and society are more inclined to seek out alternatives. If the professor offers one brand of economics as gospel, a student of independent mind will wonder if there is not some other view of things. If he is given one set of "authorities" on problems of moral concern, the same student will wonder if there are not other authorities who say something else.

The theme is a common one in the remarks of the young conservatives themselves. In an informal poll which I conducted among some 250 students, eighty per cent of the respondents said the faculties at their schools were predominantly "Liberal." "The number of students at Harvard who are conservatively inclined," says J. Alan McKay, Harvard Law, "is surprisingly large, particularly in contrast with the coloring of the faculty." Allan Brownfeld, an editor of William and Mary's publication, *The Flat Hat,* terms the new conservatism "a spontaneous rebellion against the smug conformity of Liberal pseudo-intellectualism." Similar opinions came from *Analysis,* the student conservative magazine at the University of Pennsylvania, which says: "it is becoming general knowledge that our professors are creating, with very few exceptions, anything but the much talked of 'free market place of ideas.' "

The faculty has tended to confirm students' suspicions that they are dealing with a leaden orthodoxy. "One of the most interesting aspects of the new swing toward conservatism among students," comments Bill Williams of Villanova, "is the reaction of the professors who have had a monopoly on ideas for years. They are all sons of the New Deal and seem dumbfounded when they see students becoming conservatives." Cathleen Hosey of Rosary College says: "In organizing a conservative club on campus, I met with the strongest reactions from the predominantly Liberal faculty." Some reactions of the entrenched Liberalism have gone beyond mute amazement. Daniel Harden of Minnesota recalls the results of a secondary school campaign against the United Nations. "The principal," he says, "called in my parents and asked if they had ever considered putting me under the supervision of a psychiatrist." At Pomona College, Allan Ryskind brought down the wrath of the faculty by criticizing the left-wing bias of some of his textbooks. Four years after his graduation, he says, "Pomona professors who never knew me were reviling me to some of their students." And such campaigns of attrition do not seem to be unusual. One was waged against free market economist Milton Friedman, who delivered a lecture at Purdue University. Faculty Keynesians, several of whom were in the audience, declined to challenge Friedman after his lucid presentation. But in subsequent weeks, reports Purdue conservative Bob DeMaria, "in almost every economics class, the instructor took time out to show where Friedman was wrong. . . ."

Usually such resistance, instead of discouraging the young conservatives, has whetted their appetite for battle. Given the contrary disposition of the young, the surprised and dumbfounded professors should have expected something of the sort all along. But immersed in the notion that their own orthodoxy was the quintessence of individualism, they could not conceive of rebellion against themselves.

The uprising is not at all youthful perversity. Deeper motives are involved. One such seems to be a well-founded apprehension about the way things have worked out under the Liberal stewardship. The conservative student, after all, is not operat-

ing in a vacuum. He sees about him the handiwork of Liberalism, and he does not find it pleasing. Abroad, he can observe
the menacing advance of the Soviet Union, which the Liberals
seem incapable of confronting with resolution. At home, he can
observe the rise of the domestic state, with its crushing taxes and
its latent capabilities for oppression. He can see that the bills
for vast programs of government spending are going to be paid
by someone—and it is clear that the someone is himself.

The young conservatives, as Raymond Moley has observed,
"have already grasped the wry joke that the philosophy of
spending for spending's sake will play on them. For theirs is the
generation which will reap the bitter fruit of present improvi-
dence, in taxes and inflation. And so they become, as one of
them has said, 'angry.' "*

The note of concern implied by that analysis—concern for
limiting the advance of the domestic state—is frequently
sounded in the remarks of these young people. But it is not confined to a selfish distaste for "paying the bills." The more usual
touchstones are the moral necessity of self-reliance and the
importance of individual freedom for a healthy society. "Our
conservatism," says Tom Huston of Indiana, "is not a vested
interest conservatism, but rather an intellectual one." The conservative student, explains Robert Lucock of Grove City College, understands that one gets, and should get, only what he
has worked to achieve, and thus seeks to do away with fictitious
schemes professing to supply something for nothing. That senti-

---

* John Chamberlain offers a similar comment: "Talking to the young
right-wingers at one of their functions is an illuminating experience.
Their responses to recent history are quite uncomplicated. They don't
relish looking forward to a life in which their paychecks are destined
to be hacked into by growing charges for 'social security' which they
are sure will be paid for in monstrously inflated coin some 45 years
later."

ment is echoed by John Greenagel, conservative youth leader in Minnesota. "The essence of my political philosophy," Greenagel says, "is summed up in the favorite saying of a science teacher I had in high school: 'You can never get something for nothing.'" And at the University of Richmond, law student Ulysses Joyner says he embraces conservatism "because it is the only philosophy of government which creates the atmosphere of freedom of opportunity which is necessary to the full development of individual ability."

The concern for individual freedom itself flows from a deeper source—something more than an economic calculation or even the desire for a well-ordered society. The students are impelled, in the upshot, by abstractions. Patriotism, honor, duty, as well as freedom and responsibility—these are the words most frequently found in the literature of the campus conservatives. They are armed, not merely with cussedness, but with conviction.

The movement, on my observation, corresponds closely to the analysis presented by Professor Richard Weaver in the fall of 1960 to a gathering of conservatives. "What you have to hold out," Weaver said, "is the opportunity for young people to exert themselves in the interest of some worthy goal. You can get more enthusiasm, and loyalty, and determination by putting the case on that kind of basis, then by imitating the pitch of the materialist Liberals who are our natural enemies."

And what better adversary for idealism than the contemporary monolith of "permissiveness"? Whatever else may be said for Liberalism's famed tolerance, it is not very satisfying ethically. In its insistence that everything is grey, that judgments of right and wrong should be perpetually suspended, it denies "idealism" at its source. An ideal can hardly be cherished if detachment from all values is the course of wisdom, and moral vehemence is a sign of immaturity. It is this world without value that repels the idealistic student, and sends him for counsel and consolation to the great teachings of civilized tradition.

Here is the way Carol Bauman, a leader in the conservative group, Young Americans for Freedom, expresses it:

It is not only the negative fear of oppressive taxation, the welfare state and its concurrent loss of freedoms, and the decreased material prosperity under socialism which has made American youth conservative. . . . Man's sense of 'right,' long ignored by modernist theorists, is manifesting itself in young people more than ever today through their preoccupation with principle. They have longed for a philosophy, and a unifying belief for which to fight during this protracted conflict with Communism, and they have found it in men like John Adams, Alexander Hamilton, and Edmund Burke. What appeals to them most is these men's great dedication to duty, and individual responsibility.

Charles Wessels, a student leader at Wittenberg College, believes the conservative movement is "rooted in the desire that America's young people have to recapture the ideals upon which this nation was founded. They no longer wish to indulge in the luxury of indifference."

Finally, these youngsters are highly conscious that, in their activities, conservatism has assumed the aspect of a vanguard movement. They revel in the paradox. "I am convinced that there is, indeed, a real 'thunder on the right,' " says John Price of Wabash College, "which is swiftly spreading across the nation's campuses. Someday history might record this growing movement of students as the turning point, away from the national and international decline of America." "Great numbers of our youth," writes editor Gale Pfund of the conservative journal, *Insight and Outlook,* "who lack the resignation of their elders, are seeing Liberalism as the hoax it is. . . . In the war of ideas the conservatives have now assumed the offensive and are penetrating deeply." "Campus conservatism," says Robert Richards of the University of Washington, "is gaining momentum every day." I have a sheaf of similar observations from other young conservative leaders.* One of them, Scott Stanley of the University of Kansas Law School, offers this appraisal and affirmation: "All of the alphabetical asininity which appealed so much to our parents is being recognized by fresh young minds for the hodgepodge of illogic and fallacy which it has always been. We have embarked on a great endeavor. We shall succeed."

This is the voice of revolution—eager for battle, confident of the issue, certain history is in its favor. And the confidence is supported by impressive results on individual campuses. At Wisconsin, young conservative Tony Cadden says that, "while the battle is far from won, there is a definite resurgence of conservatism among the students and a great quaking apprehension among the faculty." At Holy Cross, according to conservative leader Bill Madden, the change has been thorough and dramatic. "Conservatives now run the school and do so with a sense of purpose and direction; the newspaper, honor society, debating society have all changed their political position in the last few years."

George Decas, who has participated in the conservative movement in both the fallow and the fertile years, at Yale and then at Penn, catches the change in mood. In 1958, he recalls, exhaustive publicity efforts for an important meeting at Yale netted an audience of sixty-five people. Whereas "last Decem-

* One young conservative, Lon Woodbury of Idaho, observes that "the conservative movement is not restricted to this country, but is much more widespread. For example, as I understand it, the students in Norway are generally members of the conservative party even when it has long been out of power and is a fairly small minority."

ber, at Penn, we showed 'Operation Abolition' (with no featured speaker) to a capacity audience of about three hundred,
after only three days notice by way of posters. And in April, we
drew eight hundred to a talk by William F. Buckley."

A parallel observation comes from Edwin McDowell, a graduate of Temple, now an editorial writer with *The Arizona Republic*. "During my three years at Temple," McDowell writes,
"I didn't know another conservative, and the only two I knew
in all of Philadelphia were Vic Milione [of ISI] and Fred Nelson [an editor of the *Saturday Evening Post*]. Now I'm told
that the University of Pennsylvania, almost as Liberal as Temple, has two viable conservative organizations. And that is only
one sign. Never have I noticed people so concerned over the
failure of Liberal political and economic measures. Each day
brings encouraging news of a new campus conservative political
organization."

Thus the rudiments of rebellion: Youth's natural reaction
against the going order, apprehensions about Liberalism's
demonstrated failures, the spark of idealism, the sense of mis-
sion and the conviction of triumph. To these I would add one
more: Young people are interested in things which are bright,
lively, diverting. And the sonorous repetitions of Liberalism
are none of these. An orthodoxy, unchallenged too long, loses
its resilience. It becomes intellectually sluggish, incapable of
answering criticisms. It is dead on its feet. That, in too many
instances, seems to be the case with Liberalism today. Young
people may thus be forgiven if they have concluded that, other
issues apart, Liberalism will not do because it is a bore.

*   *   *

Granted that a "creative minority" is in rebellion, who are
the students that compose it? What kind of family back-

ground do they have? How does that background affect their beliefs—particularly as they encounter the prevailing Liberalism of the campus?

In answer to those questions, it is sometimes argued that the conservative student is one who comes from a fairly well-to-do background. If he is from a family with considerable social status, it is argued, he will naturally tend to be conservative. If he claims less opulent beginnings, he will be more inclined toward Liberalism. Thus, in keeping with the determinist views which suffuse the academy itself, the campus trend toward conservatism is sometimes attributed to "the fraternity boys."

Attempting to check the accuracy of this analysis, I conducted an informal poll of a number of young conservatives, both "student leaders" and rank and file. This effort, accomplished with the kind assistance of Miss Shirley Bullard of the Intercollegiate Society of Individualists, was not designed to support weighty generalizations about American students, or even student conservatives, as a whole. Its modest intention was simply to quiz a cross-section of young conservatives to find out who they were and where they came from. The results are not statistically conclusive; but I think they offer a rather surprising insight into what is happening on a number of American campuses.

Two questionnaires were sent out. One asked for conventional biographical data and for an estimate of the political climate the student encountered at his school. The other sought to discern the "Economic Sources of Student Conservatism." These were mailed to 265 students—93 "student leaders," and 172 "rank and file." The second form was anonymous, to avoid the possibility of the students' feeling we were trying to pry into their family circumstances.

The principal questions on the economic questionnaire concerned the student's political affiliation, his father's occupation and annual income, whether the student had a scholarship to help him through college, whether he held a job to help with his college expenses, his parents' political affiliation, whether his parents were "conservatives," "Liberals," or "neutral," and whether he considered himself more "Liberal" or less "Liberal" than his parents. Finally, the student was asked whether his parents had influenced his political beliefs.

The returns on this questionnaire, mailed to a random sample of the ISI list, were quite high. Of the 256 delivered to students, 122, or about forty-seven per cent, were returned. The overwhelming majority (85) were Republican; only seven were Democrats; thirty classed themselves as "independents."

The returns on matters of economics were surprising. Of the 122 returns, 62, or better than half, listed their family incomes in the $5,000 or under bracket. Another 39 gave their income as in the $5,000-$10,000 range; above that, returns dropped off sharply. Between $10,000 and $20,000, there were 11 students; between $20,000 and $30,000, only five; and at $50,000 and above, again only five. In other words, roughly fifty-one per cent of the students have family incomes of $5,000 or less; and 101 of the 122, or roughly eighty per cent, have family incomes of $10,000 or less.

A substantial number of the students, 51, had scholarships to help them through school, and an even higher number, 87, held jobs to help them out with their expenses. Neither of these figures can be taken as an absolute correlation with need, of course, since some scholarships are awarded purely on the basis of merit, and students hold down jobs who conceivably could get along without them. Thirty-three of the scholarship holders, however, come from the $5,000 bracket, and another 15 from the $10,000 bracket; only three came from the $20,000 and above bracket. The jobholders divide roughly along the same lines; 47 of the 87 were from the $5,000 bracket, an additional 30 from the $10,000 group. Only 10 jobholders came from families with an income of $20,000 or more.

The picture that emerges is the opposite of the "rich young fogy" sometimes conjured in discussions of the new phenomenon. The typical young conservative, in this sampling, comes from a family with an annual income of around $5,000, holds a job while in college, and is often likely to have scholarship aid in getting through school. Those results offer little or no support for the argument that student conservatism can be accounted for by economics. They do not suggest that the conservative revival has sprung from the desire to hang onto inherited wealth, or to preserve lofty status in the social scale.

The survey *does* suggest, however, that a student's parents influence his beliefs considerably. Of 121 replies to the question, "Do you believe your parents have influenced your political beliefs?" 78 respondents said "yes," 43 said "no." That answer is supported by the fact that the majority of the students identified their parents as both Republicans (76 father, 78 mother), and conservatives (81). Thus it would seem that the conservative beliefs of the parents are indeed transmitted to the students. But an interesting variation develops. More students (85) are Republican than are parents. Moreover, to the question of whether they considered themselves more or less "Liberal" than their parents, the same number said they considered themselves *less* Liberal, *more* conservative, than their parents.

The students were asked to give a brief summary of the way in which their parents had affected their political beliefs, if the student believed they had. Several, particularly among the rank and file, said they came from Republican homes, and that they had therefore always considered themselves Republicans.

Others said their parents had taught them to "think through" issues, and that this had led them to become conservatives; a smaller number said they were rebelling against parental Liberalism.

The most frequent answer, appearing regularly in the replies of the student leaders, had to do with parental training on certain fundamentals of behavior, and of attitudes toward such matters as morality, self-reliance, and patriotism.

Here are some sample answers:

Brought me up to believe in the individual and to see him as the center of society, not the state. (Father a printer; annual income $7,000.)

By teaching me the value of responsibility in the affairs of life. (Father a farmer, deceased; annual income $4,000.)

They have trained me to be responsible for my actions, self-reliant, desirous of education, believing in an absolute God, not entirely motivated by material well-being; proud of my name, nationality, country, religion, and principles of freedom and honor. (Father a tool and die maker, income $6,500 annually.)

Because I was raised on the premise that each man has the responsibility of independence and to provide for himself and his dependents. (Father a salesman, income $5,000 annually.)

I was raised a Taft Republican—and raised in the older morality of self-sufficiency, honor, etc. (Father a patent attorney, income $25,000-$30,000 annually.)

Raising me to act on my own, and giving me respect for the individual as the basis any society should be built on. (Parents writers, combined annual income of $11,000.)

Primarily in the day-to-day values which they have taught me—self-reliance, Victorian morality, rigid honesty and honor, etc. (Father, sales manager, advertising company, annual income, $10,000.)

Certainly, if nothing else, they imbued in me a strong sense of independence and have always told me that if I didn't do it for myself, it wouldn't get done; attached to this was a deep respect for that which one does for himself. Even in difficult financial times, my father has strongly opposed any government support of any kind which probably would have temporarily eased the situation. (Father a rancher, estimated annual income, $10,000.)

The manner in which I was brought up taught me that I must work hard to get ahead and success would depend on my own merits. (Father a physician, annual income, $10,000-$15,000.)

Mother was from Ireland and from early youth I was taught how the Irish fought to preserve the 'established rights' against the new, or foreign, rights of England. I always thought of my parents as being the good old-fashioned kind until I reached maturity and discovered that they were just basically conservative. (Father a railroad clerk, annual income, $5,500.)

In dashing off a hurried comment on one or the other influence which had been exerted upon him, each of these students undoubtedly selected one of many possible factors. The same families which were chalked up as "self-reliant" in these spaces were probably also Republicans, or explicitly "conservative" in their outlook. But the high incidence of the kind of answer given above suggests that this reason, more than any other, has impelled student conservatives (particularly those in positions of leadership), to take their present stand on issues. What strikes me about these answers is how closely they resemble the values of the "inner-directed" man described by David Riesman: the note of proud self-reliance, the internalized system of morality are the very hallmarks of the kind of citizen who has supposedly been vanishing from our midst.

Acknowledging the influence of their "inner-directed" parents, these students exhibit a generally hostile attitude toward their "other-directed" professors. In the companion question-naire, they were asked to say whether the climate of their school was "Liberal," "conservative," or "neutral." Ninety-nine said Liberal, 16 said conservative, and 6 said neutral. Moreover, 5 of the 16 conservative designations came from a single school (Grove City College), and were based principally upon the work of its economics department. The balance is overwhelm-ingly in favor of the Liberals. The campus environment is op-posed, according to the usual formula, to the values inculcated in the home.

Some typical comments include:

The absurdities of the so-called Liberals and their pious platitudes have served to drive me even deeper into the con-servative camp. (Indiana University)

I believe the vast majority of college and university professors are Liberals. My political science professor seemed to be one of the lonely conservatives left; he was most fair in presenting both sides of a question. (Ripon College)

Rockford College has an extremely "Liberal" climate. This is one of the reasons for our recent formation of a discussion group. I feel that in too many cases professors are dwelling on theoretical, scientific sounding statements of opinion, rather than on objective fact.

The climate at both my universities is quite Liberal and I found that usually I was one of a very few people representing the conservative point of view. I try when possible to encourage people to read conservative books and think about the long-range effects of Liberalism. (From a graduate of Western Re-serve, BA, and Wayne State University, MA)

Antioch College, of course, is noted for its Liberal approach. I find this is true in almost all lectures, assemblies, and attitude of administration. Government courses, especially, are slanted (perhaps the profs stopped learning in the 1940s) toward New Dealism and centralism.

The climate at the University of Minnesota is extremely Liberal. The only Republican in the political science department admits to being more Liberal than Governor Rockefeller and half of the Democrats. A conscious effort is constantly made by instructors to liberalize the thinking of their students.

I was a conservative basically before I came to college, but the exceedingly Liberal atmosphere has led me to independent study and a stronger conservatism. (Rosary College)

I happened to major in political science at Notre Dame, which has a conservative department. The rest of the liberal arts school is overwhelmingly Liberal in typical fashion. In those courses not taught by political scientists I generally became quite annoyed.

At UCR, the political science, history, and economics departments range from moderate Liberals to Marxian socialists. I enjoy attending a Liberal school. I feel as if I grow in this hard environment in a Toynbeean challenge-and-response sense. (University of California, Riverside)

The University of Maryland is secularistic and relativistic, and is very Liberal. However, there do exist many people on the campus who articulate both the conservative and the libertarian point of view.

Liberal-neutral, anti-conservatism. Not vigorously Liberal, but certainly anti-conservative in general. Naturally, there are exceptions to this generalization. (Marquette)

These opinions do not, incidentally, represent the attitude of students who have an axe to grind against the faculty. All of these quotations are taken from the remarks of students who have received academic honors—Dean's List, *cum laude,* Phi Beta Kappa.

In dealing with the Liberal environment, the young conservatives have frequent recourse to conservative literature. Asked to name the source which has influenced them *most* in their thinking, many give joint credit to their parents and to independent study. But "independent study" is cited altogether much more frequently (92 respondents) than is parental influence (53 respondents). Considering the fact that most of these students acknowledge coming from conservative homes, the imbalance in favor of "independent study" may be in part owing to a natural desire to profess intellectual self-sufficiency. But the sources cited by these students suggest they do engage in study of their own, and quite a bit of it.

Asked to name individuals or publications that have been most effective in crystallizing their views, the students pointed to two influences in particular—Senator Barry Goldwater and his book, *The Conscience of a Conservative* (24 respondents), and William F. Buckley, Jr., and *National Review* magazine (20 respondents). Buckley and Goldwater, polemicist and politician, are clearly the two major heroes of these collegians. Asked to cite the materials which they read most frequently, the students singled out *National Review* (74), *Time* (50), *US News and World Report* (40), publications from ISI (35), *Human Events* (30), *Newsweek* (29), publications from FEE (26), *The Wall Street Journal* (20), and *Modern Age* (18). Besides Buckley and Goldwater, the two "influences" most frequently cited were the Intercollegiate Society of Individualists (11) and author Russell Kirk (10).

It seems to me from these reflections that the young conservative movement is essentially dissimilar to conventional notions of rebellion—zealous son rebelling against stodgy father. The typical young conservative emerging from this survey is quite faithful to the values of his parents, and indeed tends to be more articulate and aggressive than they about defending them. Rather than a revolt of generation against generation, then, the young conservative uprising would seem to be the work of an "inner-directed underground"—a generation of parents who, in an age of other-direction, have held fast to traditional values, and bootlegged them to their children. The children have then carried those values into the community, done battle for them, and in the course of that battle become more solidified in their conservatism.

Viewed in the aggregate, the uprising may seem simply to be, as Lionel Trilling believes, the backward motion of the pendulum; but it is in fact a reversal of that stereotype. In the old pattern, a youngster would be brought up in a traditionalist home, then go away to school, there to be taken into camp by the glib generalizations of the professoriate. In the new pattern, the youngster receives certain values from his parents, and contests the Liberalism of his professors.

The crucial difference, partially justifying the pendulum analogy, is the fact that, in the first instance, the student's parents were at one with the prevailing mood of the society, his professors opposed to it; today, the professors are the voices of conformity, and the student finds the values his parents taught him in a decided minority. He can at once vindicate the traditional values of the "inner-directed" and enjoy the youthful kick of rebellion against the going order.

The large number of students who identify their parents as "conservative," or of the old-school, suggests that, if our society had gone as completely toward other-direction as some collectivists had wished, there would not be a conservative uprising today. But, as Riesman notes, areas of "inner-direction" have remained. Without the teachings of their parents, these students would have neither an alternative position to defend, nor the granitic self-reliance required to do battle with professors, the majority of the student population, and the influences of the mass media.

The conservative uprising today, on the evidence of this survey, owes a great deal to a band of "inner-directed" Americans who somehow managed to hang onto the old values while the rest of society was drifting into other-direction. The present campus movement is the work, not simply of generation against generation, but of "inner-directed" generations working in harness against a hostile society.

III

ISI

"Aren't all economists Keynesians?"

MC GEORGE BUNDY, former Dean of the
Harvard faculty, quoted by Chesly Manly

FOR ALL THE TALK of reaction against conformity, a rebellion is not so easily made. The very characteristics which
make conformity oppressive make it difficult to dislodge. Those
in power are not anxious to make way for their opponents, and
tend to encourage the view that the *status quo* is part of the
natural order of life—that alternatives to it, in Professor Richard Weaver's phrase, are not "on the agenda of discussable
things."

For these reasons, the most depressing part of being a conservative student is the feeling, artfully enforced by the opposition, that one is so terribly alone. On the other side are all the
"authorities:" the prevailing attitudes in government, the
ranked expertise of the faculty, most student publications, the
textbooks, the *apparat* of the intelligentsia, periodicals, newspapers, the facile commentaries of the electronic media. Against
all this, the conservative student, down through the years, has
nurtured a presentiment that something is wrong. He has been

game for rebellion, but the pressures surrounding him have worked against his achieving it. Thanks to a reign of psychological intimidation—which has even been carried to the point of suggesting that people of conservative instinct are mentally unbalanced*—the potential rebel is likely, unless receiving some powerful encouragement, to keep his opinions to himself. And the nodal point of revolution comes only when the urge for self-expression and protest becomes stronger than the urge for security and acceptance.

The preceding chapter has stressed the importance, in the conservative rebellion, of alternative sources of value. Without the fortification of parental teachings and conservative literature, the conservative impulse in all likelihood would not be brought to full expression. If student misgivings are to be consummated in revolution, rather than attenuated in self-doubt and timidity, someone has to take on the job of sustaining a mood of defiance. The key to the conservative uprising has thus been the development of an intellectual community to provide alternatives to the Liberal orthodoxy, and of an agency to unite that community with the prospective rebels.

Fortunately, the forces of other-direction have not occupied every citadel in our society, although they have certainly captured the decisive centers of power. In spite of the massive commitment of most American "intellectuals" to the prevailing ethic, several pockets of resistance do exist. As things now stand, these are essentially three: Old-line opponents of statism, who have remained steadfast to the principles of the Western tradition throughout the Liberal ascendancy—men like Ludwig von Mises and F. A. Hayek in economics, Eric Voegelin and Leo

---

* See, e.g., *The Authoritarian Personality,* by T. W. Adorno et al; *The New American Right,* Daniel Bell, ed; *Revolt of the Moderates,* by Samuel Lubell.

Strauss in political and moral philosophy. The defectors—those who had accepted leftist ideas, who had been "wrong for the right reasons"—but who became disillusioned with radical doctrine; men like Eugene Lyons and James Burnham, Max Eastman and Whittaker Chambers. The new wave, those who had been educated during the Liberal reign, but with whom, for some reason, the vaccination failed to take. These include men like Russell Kirk and Stanley Parry, Hans Sennholz and Ben Rogge, Bill Buckley and Brent Bozell.

These scholars and journalists were divided in other ways as well; ideologically, chronologically, geographically; each was at work in his own *metier,* picking his way through the maze of Liberal error, seeking out old truths and modern applications. Communications among them were poor; opportunities for publication were infrequent; but gradually, they began producing a new literature of freedom, vindicating the historic values of the West, resurrecting the forgotten laws of the free market, dissecting the strategic follies of our default to Communism. And they began to reclaim the great writings of the conservative tradition, and to bring them once more into public repute: Burke, Acton, Tocqueville, Madison, Adams, Calhoun, Burckhardt, Babbitt, More.

Through the efforts of conservative publishers like Henry Regnery, Devin-Adair, and the Caxton printers, these writers began to establish a market for themselves. By 1960, their efforts had proceeded so far as to produce a virtual flowering of conservative literature: John Chamberlain, Russell Kirk, Bill Buckley, Thomas Molnar, Felix Morley, Henry Hazlitt, Richard LaPiere, Richard Weaver, William Henry Chamberlin, Ralph de Toledano, Frank Meyer—all these and others published books of primary consequence.

In the meantime, a number of organizations had been bring-

ing out pamphlets and studies supporting the conservative view
—the Foundation for Economic Education, the American Economic Foundation, the American Enterprise Association.

The existence of a literature served to confederate these various scholars into a "community." And with its development,
conservatism also developed a journalism of its own, which both
signified and abetted the rise of a new conservative republic of
letters.

The standby publication for conservatives, down through
the years and through many permutations, has been *The Freeman*. Established in the 1920s by Albert Jay Nock, it was resur-
rected in the early 50s by a group of libertarians, conservatives
and anti-Communists.* John Chamberlain, Henry Hazlitt, Forrest Davis, Suzanne LaFollette, James Burnham, and Max Eastman all acted as "editor"—officially and unofficially—during this
phase of its existence. In 1954, the magazine was passed over to
the Foundation for Economic Education. Frank Chodorov, an
old friend of Nock's, was introduced as its new editor, and
served in that capacity until late in 1955. Today *The Freeman*
is still published by FEE, with its primary emphases on economics and libertarian arguments against the state.

Chodorov had come to *The Freeman* from *Human Events,* a
weekly newsletter which for many years was the only conservative publication going. *Human Events* had been founded in
1944 by Frank Hanighen (a former correspondent for the old
New York Post), Henry Regnery, and Felix Morley. Beginning
from a small circulation, *Human Events* has blossomed into the
largest-circulation conservative journal, with around fifty-thou-
sand readers. Its executive publisher, who has adroitly used
direct-mail and other promotional techniques to help the pub-

* A revival stimulated by the brief, intense existence of Alfred Kohl-
berg's magazine, *Plain Talk*.

lication attain this figure, is James L. Wick, who came to *Human Events* in 1953.

In 1955, when *The Freeman* shifted to a greater emphasis on economics, conservatism developed another effective counterweight to the intellectual appeal of *The Nation* and the *New Republic*. Bill Buckley, after an arduous year of fund-raising, launched his *National Review,* which in 1960 celebrated, before an illustrious gathering of more than one thousand souls, an unexpected fifth birthday. *National Review* has served as a frequent outlet for conservative writers, acquainted them with one another's work, and developed new talent. It has become an intellectual journal which can meet the Liberals on their own ground.

Contrary to the notion that conservatives are illiterate curmudgeons, a survey of the NR clientele established that more of its readers attended college than did readers of the *New Yorker* (76 to 75.3 per cent), and more attended graduate school (35 per cent) than did the highly selected audience of *Business Week* (21 per cent).

In 1956 came a fourth journal, even more explicitly pitched to the level of the intellectual community, equally determined to establish the philosophical foundations upon which political and social behavior should be premised. Entitled *Modern Age,* this journal is now approaching the ten thousand level in circulation—a formidable figure for a magazine devoted exclusively to matters of philosophy, history, and the arts.

While this growing literature formed a "community" in the intellectual sense, its components were physically scattered— particularly in the early years of development. By the early 1950s, the answers to Liberal doctrine had been, or were being, formulated and put to paper. But for the most part they reposed in isolated books or monographs. Here or there a professor had hacked through the sophistries of positivist sociology, Keynesian economics, challenging jurisprudence. Mises held forth at New York University, Parry at Notre Dame, Vivas at Northwestern, Hayek and Friedman at Chicago; their labors formed a small and diffused corpus of doctrine not readily found in most college libraries. What political science course canvassed the teachings of Eric Voegelin? How many economics departments acknowledged the existence, much less the merit, of the Austrian school? How many sociology students were familiar with the devastating critique of sociological impudence conducted by such as Pitirim Sorokin and Richard Weaver?

The students needed access to this conservative authority; they needed the tools of intellectual discrimination, the substance of effective argument—facts, analysis, expertise. To supply that need, a suitable intermediary was soon to appear.

Nineteen fifty-three might in a number of respects be considered the watershed year for the rise of conservatism among American college students. It was in that year that Russell Kirk published *The Conservative Mind,* which burst upon the nation's intelligentsia as a perplexing and embarrassing challenge. In the teeth of Liberal assertions that conservatives are superannuated and inarticulate, Kirk hurled a monumental defense of the conservative philosophy. He was young (then thirty-five); he was obviously well-read; and he wrote with an eloquence and power that could be neither ridiculed nor ignored.

In that same year, in a small office in northwest Washington, a group was formed which was to take the elements of revolution and compose them into a serious and effective movement. The organization was called "The Intercollegiate Society of Individualists." Its function was to distribute literature to college students—to get into their hands the theories and the information being marshalled by the new intellectual community.

The founder and president of ISI is Frank Chodorov, a veteran journalist and activist in the cause of freedom. Then in his sixties, Chodorov recalled the early years of this century, when the Socialists began their patient seduction of the American mind. He had observed the radical movement closely, and he knew the stress it placed on enlisting the sympathies of the young. He was particularly in mind of a group called the Intercollegiate Socialist Society, an organization which, although most Americans today have never heard of it, worked a lasting influence on the national destiny.

The ISS began, purely as a campus venture, in 1905. Its first president was the novelist, Jack London. Its purpose, "to awaken an interest in Socialism among the educated men and women of the country." In this it succeeded beyond all expectations. It so effectively spread its doctrines among "the educated" that today it can claim as alumni some of the most powerful opinion makers in the United States. These include labor leaders David Dubinsky, Al Hayes, Andrew Biemiller, Jay Lovestone, Walter and Victor Reuther; academicians Leonard Doob, Talcott Parsons, Harold Faulkner, and Sidney Hook; journalists Murray Kempton, Max Lerner, James Wechsler, and Joe Lash (all of the *New York Post*), Freda Kirchwey, Bruce Bliven, Walter Lippmann; and government servants Ralph Bunche and Paul Porter.

Lippmann gave this summary of his group's objectives at Harvard: "In a general way our object was to make reactionaries standpatters; standpatters, conservative liberals; conservative liberals and liberals, radicals; and radicals, Socialists. In other words, we tried to move everyone up a peg. . . . We preferred to have the whole mass move a little, to having a few move altogether out of sight." To judge from the present state of Harvard, Lippman's effort must be accounted a brilliant success. And he and his colleagues have since performed a like service for the rest of the country. They have gone forth into the world to shape its opinions and its policies—and those opinions and policies, over the years, have come more and more to resemble the attitudes of ISS.

The root of the matter, Chodorov believed, was the planting of "collectivist seed . . . in the soft and fertile student mind forty-odd years ago." Viewing the Socialists' handiwork from the perspective of a half-century, he declared that "the outstanding occurrence of the preceding fifty years had been the transmutation of the American character from individualist to collectivist." But what had been learned could be unlearned; or, more precisely, the old values of freedom could be learned, as something "new," by new generations.

"We are not born with ideas," Chodorov wrote in *Human Events,* "we learn them. If Socialism has come to America because it was implanted in the minds of past generations, there is no reason for assuming that the contrary idea cannot be taught to a new generation. What the Socialists have done can be undone, if there is a will for it. But the undoing will not be accomplished by trying to destroy established Socialist institutions. It can be accomplished only by attacking minds, and not the minds of those already hardened by Socialistic fixations."

That article was the beginning of ISI. A businessman read it. He sent Chodorov a check for $1,000 to get "freedom" clubs, or something of the sort, started on American campuses. Then, Chodorov recalls, "I happened to visit the Foundation for Economic Education and mentioned . . . the check. Ivan Bierly [executive secretary] . . . said that if I got the names of students who would read libertarian literature, the Foundation would be glad to send them their pamplets. That seemed to me a sound idea. I had had in mind the sending out of an organizer, but the literature idea had the advantage of getting the students to select themselves. So I went back to Washington and incorporated the Intercollegiate Society of Individualists. I sent out a letter to readers of *Human Events,* asking for names of students who might be interested in such literature, and about six hundred came in." ISI was set up as a mailing-list operation in the offices of *Human Events,* and began sending out publications from FEE.

Such were the modest biginnings of 1953. In the eight years since, they have been extended, not by high-pressure campaigning, but by the slow accretion of consent. If this was, as Chodorov conceived it, a war for individual minds, it could be won only by the capillary movement of ideas—movement which takes place only as quickly as individual volition will let it. The ISI student, first of all, must have a desire for something different, something in contrast to the collectivist orthodoxy; he must have a spontaneous sympathy for the philosophy of freedom and the kind of intellect that spurns simplistic fallacies, and opens into the deeper logic of free men and free institutions.

For these reasons, ISI stresses its own voluntarism; it has made no effort to dragoon unwilling students into reading its literature. Every recipient is self-selected, receiving mailings only if he wants them. With the literature, students receive a card which can be filled out and sent in by interested colleagues, or else returned to ISI removing them from the mailing list, if they so desire.

By these low-pressure methods, ISI has in the space of eight years built its mailing list from six hundred to better than thirteen thousand. An estimated forty thousand students have benefited from its efforts to mediate between conservative scholars and restive collegians. Among the materials it has sent out are such books as Felix Morley's *Freedom and Federalism;* Buckley's and Bozell's *McCarthy and His Enemies;* Kirk's *The Conservative Mind;* Frederic Bastiat's *The Law;* Chodorov's *Rise and Fall of Society;* Richard Weaver's *Ideas Have Consequences;* Henry Hazlitt's *Economics in One Lesson;* Hayek's *Road to Serfdom;* Ludwig von Mises' *Human Action.*

ISI has undertaken an ambitious publications program of its own, including a newsletter called *The Individualist,* a number of philosophical monographs, booklets, and numerous reprints. Among ISI's own publications are *Those Who Would Have Freedom From Tyranny,* by Dr. Ralph Cooper Hutchinson; *Religion and the Social Problem,* by Rev. Edmund A. Opitz; *Education for What?* by Dr. Charles Coulter and Richard Rimanoczy; *The Sociological Perspective* and *The Integrity of the Person,* by A. H. Hobbs; a monograph on natural law, by Opitz and Edward Barrett; two volumes of *The Admiral's Log,* by Admiral Ben Moreell; *Education and the Individual* and *Relativism and the Crisis of Our Times,* by Weaver; and *The Wonderful World of Modern Economics,* by Prof. William H. Peterson.

Included in its numerous reprints and publications purchased from others are works by Gerhart Niemeyer, David McCord Wright, William F. Buckley, Jr., Frank S. Meyer, and Sylvester Petro.

The boom in paperback books has not been overlooked. The increasing availability of important literature in this form—both contemporary work and conservative classics—has made the paperback an important vehicle for getting information to students. Consequently, ISI has established what it calls its "Paperback Bookshelf"—a selection of literature, covering the most important aspects of conservative philosophy, available in these low-priced editions. Among the selections are *Ideas Have Consequences,* Kirk's *Prospects for Conservatives,* Mises' *Planning for Freedom,* and *The Road to Serfdom.*

Students have responded enthusiastically to these offerings. "The ISI was of immense value to me," wrote a student at the University of Michigan. "Here on campus we are subjected to a barrage of Liberal propaganda, from Keynesian economics to Big Government political science. Textbooks, to a greater or lesser degree, are slanted." Another student wrote: "This year our debate topic concerned economic aid, and your publications certainly helped me in both debate and extemporaneous speaking." A senior at Rice said the literature helped him probe the doctrines being handed down in class. A student at the Colorado School of Mines wrote: "This is a very fine program. It gave me heart just when I thought that there was no hope of an individualistic opposition in this country."

As its functions expanded, ISI moved out of its borrowed headquarters, first at *Human Events* and later with FEE, to its own offices in Philadelphia. ISI now holds forth from 410 Lafayette Building—on Independence Square, right across from the building where the Constitution was conceived. The group has also opened an active Midwest branch in Indianapolis (1014 Lemcke Building), which has helped galvanize conservative students in Ohio, Indiana, Illinois, Michigan, and Wisconsin. ISI has sparked such student publications as the *New Individualist Review* at the University of Chicago, *Insight and Outlook* at the University of Wisconsin, and *Analysis* at the University of Pennsylvania. It has arranged for speaking tours by such conservative lecturers as Frank Meyer, L. Brent Bozell, William F. Buckley, Jr., and Russell Kirk. It has held seminars featuring noted conservative scholars like Stanley Parry, Rich-

ard Weaver, Rev. Edward Keller, Dean Ben Rogge, Anthony
Bouscaren, Sylvester Petro, Hayek, Meyer, and Opitz.

In 1960 ISI launched a "summer school" designed to bring
young conservatives together, and to give some systematic atten-
tion to key problems of political philosophy. Lecturer for the
first week was Dr. David McCord Wright, speaking on "The
Moral Basis of a Free Society." He was followed by Russell
Kirk ("History and the Western Tradition"), Dr. Karl Cerny
("The American Constitution and Federalism"), and Dr. Stefan
Possony ("The Nature of Communism, Socialism, and Fas-
cism"). The reaction of one student participant, Miss Annette
Courtemanche, will suggest the impact of this enterprise.
"Here," she wrote in her school paper, "were responsive students fired with enthusiasm for preserving our freedom and
anxious to defend their beliefs. The one thing an observer
could not help but notice was how well-informed these students
were on contemporary crises. Their 'awareness' was astonishing
in an apathetic age."

Impresario of these varied activities is a former executive of
the Americans for the Competitive Enterprise System, E. Victor
Milione. At thirty-seven, Vic Milione has invested nearly half
his life in conservative advocacy. Reflective and philosophical,
he has given ISI a hard-won continuity through years of strait-
ened finances, and lent it the strength of his own deeply-
conceived convictions. Chodorov recalls: "I hired Vic Milione
to run the outfit and to visit schools in the East. . . . I told him,
'Vic, I have this money and as long as it lasts, you will get
$75 a week and expense money. You'll have to take your chances
on the future.' In due time, the $6,000 was spent and Vic worked
without salary and without expenses, until he could raise some
more money."

With Chodorov, Milione insists that the battle is primarily

one of ideas; he believes the philosophy of freedom must be clarified, deepened, annealed, before a successful movement can take place. He has labored to give ISI a philosophical timbre not usually found in organizations dealing with the young. He gives this expression of ISI's conservative position:

/ A conservative is primarily one who wishes to preserve a continuity between the time-tested and consequently proven values and institutions of the past, the aspirations of the present, and the morally legitimate claims of the future. He believes that only by building on the experience and wisdom of the past—by adding the insights and experience of our own generation—can we secure greater possibilities for individual freedom, true progress and happiness for our own and future generations. . . . A conservative does not seek to preserve the past without qualification. Although he is wary of change, particularly radical change, which often is an indiscriminate break with the past, he welcomes and encourages modifications and refinements of earlier thought and institutions when they make a positive contribution toward the accomplishment of a civilized society of free men.

The basic premises of conservatism would be, in my estimation, that this is a God-created universe; that man is a part of that creation; man has a free will and a reason. From this follows the conservative's belief that individual men should be their own agents in all things respecting their own lives.

Since late 1959, Milione has been assisted in his organizational efforts by his hard-driving Midwest Director, Don Lipsett. Lipsett, now thirty, operates from a small, literature-laden office in downtown Indianapolis. His weeks are spent in roaming Midwest highways from college to college, counseling students forming new groups, advising them on campus battles with Liberaldom, supplying literature, arranging for lectures by conservative speakers. Approximately two dozen new student conservative clubs have sprung from his efforts, among them groups at Indiana University, DePauw, Earlham, Purdue, Ohio

State, Antioch, Chicago, Michigan State, Wabash, Marian College, Kenyon, Rockford, Carleton, and the State University of
Iowa.

"Our big problem now," he says, "is keeping up with the
volume of requests for literature and speakers. When we opened
the Midwest office in November 1959, I often spent two or
three days at a school looking for a capable student interested
in heading up a conservative group—one with leadership ability
as well as conservative conviction. Now clubs are springing up
so rapidly, and new leaders are developing so fast, that it's a
full time job just keeping up correspondence with them. More
reports of conservative activity now come in every week than
I used to get in a month."

A lingering difficulty, Lipsett adds, concerns the matter of
getting faculty sponsorship. Some schools are so thoroughly
Liberal that no faculty member can be found to sponsor a conservative group. "College trustees and alumni," he says, "are
frequently told how conservative the faculty is at their school.
Yet at a number of colleges students in search of an advisor—
usually required by school regulations—have trouble finding
even one who will stand up and be counted as a conservative."

As Lipsett carries to the students the teachings and the literature of the Philadelphia office, he keeps national headquarters
closely tuned in on developments on midland campuses. The
success of this tandem operation is such that the Philadelphia
headquarters is now at work to set up a similar regional office
on the West Coast.

While the zeal of its student members has carried it increasingly into formal organizational efforts, ISI has stuck faithfully
to its educational, voluntary program. It makes no attempt
either to discipline or control the student groups affiliated with
it—in notable contrast to some Liberal youth organizations. It

simply tries to supply literature, advice, and inspiration; and depends on student initiative to take it from there. As one issue of *The Individualist* put it: "ISI issues no 'charter' and makes no attempt to control the activities of its chapters, although it will gladly assist them in any way it can. The programs undertaken to forward conservatism at the various schools are left to the initiative and the discretion of the students on the scene."

As a result of this emphasis on student volition, ISI groups sport a wide variety of names. The most common—as at Wisconsin and Michigan State—is "Conservative Club." Some, as at the University of Chicago, call themselves the such-and-such chapter of ISI. Others are named after noted conservatives or have titles suited to their particular campuses. Examples: The Robert A. Taft Club of Queens College, the Eleutherian Society (Penn), the Whiggamores (Ohio State), the George Washington Club (original name of DePauw's conservative club), Society for Individual Insight (Purdue), Society for Conservative Studies (Pitt). Almost every name has been used that comports with local tradition, youthful invention, and collegiate flair for the unusual. ISI has thus established a loose confederation of student conservatives, groups and individuals, concerned to restore America's traditional regard for individual freedom, each in the way most appropriate to local circumstances.

Like many another young organization—indeed, like the Socialist group whose influence it seeks to annul—ISI has not been without its troubles. One of the primary difficulties has been financial; a program geared to long-range effects does not have an easy time of it raising funds. Whereas there are numerous large foundations of Liberal hue which may be counted on to sustain and subsidize youth efforts on the left, there are few willing to perform the same service for conservatives. ISI's mod-

est budget* has been met, in large part, by individual contributions of moderate size. Now, with growing interest in the conservatism of young people, more potential contributors are
beginning to realize the value of supporting educational work
among the young. But the task, even with ISI's tax-deductible
status, is still not an easy one, as Vic Milione heartily testifies.

Another difficulty has centered on the question of ISI's name.
Because the group is dedicated, as its letterhead puts it, to "the
advancement of conservative thought on the campus," there
has been considerable discussion among ISI backers about alter-
ing the name. A "society of individualists," it is argued, suggests
something a little different from the philosophy of conservatism.
For one thing, "individualism," in the philosophical sense, has
been associated with the teachings of Mill, Spencer, and the
classical liberals of the 19th century. Its roots are positivist, secular, utilitarian.

This is not, however, the philosophical character of ISI. Its
president, Frank Chodorov, is indeed an individualist of the
"rugged" variety, a devotee of Locke and Adam Smith. He
sometimes refers to his position on social matters as approaching that of "philosophic anarchy"—a rejection, on principle, of
the authority of the state, a bias in favor of the uncoerced man.

But Chodorov's position, on analysis, is not the secular hu-
manism of the nineteenth century. It is grounded, not in a
utilitarian calculus, but in religious conviction, a respect for
the integrity of personality, and a mistrust of aggregated power.
The dual emphasis of his philosophy, and of ISI's, is to affirm
the authority of value, and the autonomy of the individual arising from it.

ISI's publications everywhere reflect this emphasis—as in

* $100,000 in 1960.

A. H. Hobbs' monograph, *The Integrity of the Person,* Frank Meyer's *Freedom, Tradition, Conservatism,* Richard Weaver's *Conservatism and Libertarianism: The Common Ground,* or in Milione's affirmation that ours is a "God-created" universe in which man has been made free to choose between good and evil. Vindication of individual freedom is the secular result of ISI's educational efforts; by this definition it is indeed concerned with "individualism." But its intellectual roots are not "individualist" in the accepted philosophical sense.

The discussion suggests that the "conservative" camp comprises ideas of many hues—ranging from Nock, Mill, and Spencer on the one hand, to Eric Voegelin, Russell Kirk, and Stanley Parry on the other. That such variations exist should not, in the larger sense, be cause for dismay; philosophically, the imperatives of moral authority and secular freedom may be composed into a consistent whole, just as moral dissolution and statist compulsions may be. And, in any event, it is clear that one of the prime tasks of all conservatives is to rebuke the advance of the collectivist state. The "individualist" in ISI's title stresses the primary goal of the conservative movement in the world of politics and economics, if not in the world of moral philosophy.

IV

A Study in Loyalty

"Why does the country which is the leader of
the 'free world' produce citizens who appear to
know neither the meaning of freedom nor the
imperative loyalty which freedom demands?"

RAYMOND ENGLISH

A PRINCIPAL INGREDIENT of the Liberal conformity is
detachment from American institutions and traditions. As the
Lazarsfeld-Thielens survey indicates, faculty permissiveness
tends to reject the complex of sympathies and attachments
usually identified as "patriotism." "Flag-waving," or "jingoism,"
is considered *infra dig* among academicians, who incline to see
merit in the customs and aspirations of other cultures.

This characteristic relativism accounts for such typical faculty
opinion as devotion to supranational formulae for handling
the affairs of nations; distaste for agencies engaged in defending
American sovereignty, or imposing sanctions upon those who
would subvert it; a readiness to entertain exotic creeds and
"heresies"; and profound opposition to formal affirmations of
"loyalty" to the United States.*

* This point is discussed at greater length in the Epilogue, "Academic
Freedom," Part I.

74

Thus it was not surprising that, in the fall of 1959, the academic community unleashed a full-scale attack against the "loyalty oath" provisions of the National Defense Education Act. The presidents of Yale and Harvard, and of several other schools, announced they would not partake of the benefits of the law, because they found its provisions requiring recipients to affirm their loyalty to the United States, and to deny subversive affiliations, offensive to their notions of "academic freedom."

The National Defense Education Act was passed in 1958, in the wave of consternation following the announcement of Moscow's first "sputniks." N.D.E.A. was designed as a program of loans to individual students, allegedly to boost American progress in fields relevant to technical progress; hence the words "national defense" in its title. Part of the "national defense" sections of the Act required an oath of loyalty to the United States, and a "disclaimer affidavit," forswearing connection with any Communist or similar subversive group, to be signed by recipients of the allocated funds.*

Harvard and Yale withdrew from the program simultaneously, but the verbal honors went to Yale. In an article in *The New York Times Magazine,* Yale President A. Whitney Griswold launched the publicity attack. The loyalty stipulations, he argued, were "discriminatory": "The colleges and universities"

---

* The oath reads as follows: "I, _____, do solemnly swear (or affirm) that I will bear true faith and allegiance to the United States of America and will support and defend the Constitution and laws of the United States of America against all its enemies, foreign and domestic."

The affidavit reads: "I, _____, do solemnly swear (or affirm) that I do not believe in, and am not a member of and do not support any organization that believes in or teaches the overthrow of the United States government by force or violence or by any illegal or unconstitutional methods."

did not see "why their students and faculties should be treated differently from any other individuals, groups, professions, or occupations that receive federal subsidies or loans." Moreover, these provisions discriminated against individual students, because "only those who need financial assistance are required to take the affidavit and oath." Griswold's arguments were immediately taken up by other educators, and by a number of lawmakers in Congress. Senator John Kennedy had, in the previous session, introduced S. 2929, aimed at repealing the offending clause. Synods of Liberal educators denounced the loyalty provisions, and a barrage of letters began descending on the Eighty-Sixth Congress, urging passage of Kennedy's bill. The press was burdened with denunciations of the oath. As the new session got under way, the betting odds in Washington heavily favored repeal.

Some American college students, however, had different ideas. In mid-December 1959, as the repeal campaign rolled toward a crescendo, two students sat discussing the issue in a restaurant on Washington's Wisconsin Avenue. Their view of the matter, in David Riesman's terminology, was profoundly "inner-directed." They did not share the mood of academic detachment from American institutions. They rather straightforwardly professed the principles upon which the nation was founded, and viewed loyalty to the United States, not as an embarrassing parochialism, but as a sentiment worthy of proud affirmation.

On the table before the two students lay an issue of the *Washington Post,* containing the day's dispatches on the progress of the repeal campaign. The campaign, they found, was going swimmingly.

"What we need," said one of the students in disgust, "is a student committee *for* the loyalty oath."

His companion looked up from the newspaper. "Why don't we start one?"

In that half-jocular exchange, the conservative movement among young people in America took a giant step forward. As a result, the two students set about the next day to establish a "National Student Committee for the Loyalty Oath," an enterprise that portended a new departure for American politics.

The two collegians were Douglas Caddy, then a student at Georgetown University, and David Franke, a student at George Washington. Fortunately for their undertaking, they were both young men of initiative and perseverance, and, having lived and worked in Washington, conversant in the special folkways of the Capital.

If the "loyalty oath" provisions were to be saved, they knew, a strong grass-roots campaign had to be mounted in their behalf. At the time, there was little agitation, if any, in favor of retention. Someone had to convince Congress there were votes—as well as principles—to be lost if the oath and affidavit were repealed. They also knew nothing could be quite so effective as having students themselves defend the loyalty clause; they were, after all, the people called upon to sign it.

Caddy and Franke began contacting other like-minded young people around the country. They drew largely upon acquaintances made through ISI, of which they were both members, and the Young Republicans, for their first approaches. (Caddy was then State Chairman of the District of Columbia College Young Republicans; Franke was editor of both *The Individualist,* ISI's newsletter, and *The Campus Republican,* official publication of the national College Young Republicans.) They exhorted their friends to establish pro-loyalty oath chapters on individual campuses, and, where possible, at the state level. By the end of January 1960, their efforts had proceeded far enough for them to make a formal announcement of their intentions. In its first press release, the National Student Committee for the Loyalty Oath announced no less than thirty colleges represented by students on its governing board, ranging from Yale and Harvard in the East, to Antioch and Wisconsin in the Midwest, to the University of New Mexico in the West.

The wire services snapped it up. It was not quite Man Bites Dog, but Student Bites Liberalism would do. The news of this oddity was flashed out across the nation. And suddenly, with national attention focused on it, students across the nation flocked to join the affray. The Student Congress of Holy Cross came out in behalf of the loyalty provisions. A meeting of Young Republican leaders in Madison, Wisconsin, declared: "American university officials could better spend their time in combatting Communism than in attacking those who are trying to stop its advances." In Michigan, a student at the Detroit College of Law launched a statewide committee to agitate in behalf of the oath. In Texas, the University of Houston House of Representatives declared: "Any student or individual who desires to obtain such loans should be required to take an oath that he or she is not a Communist and does not advocate the overthrow of our government." At Wabash, senior Grant Van Horne established a pro-loyalty oath committee. At Clark College in Washington, the student newspaper said: "We still think no student seeking financial help from the government should object to professing his loyalty." At Mt. St. Mary's College, the student editor observed that: "If the oath is discriminatory in singling out students instead of farmers, dependent people and others who receive aid, in so doing it actually places intelligence above the other . . . on a higher plane. By singling out students, the government acknowledges the scholar's power and influence." At Valparaiso, Young Republican leader Chuck Rau spoke out in behalf of the loyalty provisions. At Davidson College in North Carolina, the *Davidsonian* allowed that the real infringement on freedom was that imposed by college administrations which denied their students the freedom to sign the oath or not, as they wished.

The rise of pro-loyalty oath sentiment among students brought similar expressions from conservative faculty members. President Kevin McCann of Defiance College, Ernest van den Haag of Columbia, Prof. Richard Martin Lyon of Notre Dame, Dr. George Soule, Maj. Gen. E. N. Harmon of Norwich University, Prof. E. Merrill Root, President V. R. Edman of Wheaton College, Dr. Edmund Zawacki of the University of Wisconsin, Rev. Robert F. Grewen, S. J., of Lemoyne College, President John T. Fey of the University of Vermont, Dr. George S. Benson of Claremont College, Dr. Robert L. Johnson, Chancellor of Temple University, and President Ernest L. Wilkinson of Brigham Young University were among those coming forward with statements of support.

Dr. McCann offered this comment on the attitude of students at his school: "Dr. A. Whitney Griswold has raised a standard around which many will gladly rally. I cannot. In raising it I think he violates the freedoms he espouses. Certainly at my own college there are students of a genuine—even if old-fashioned—loyalty, who are perfectly willing to profess this loyalty and who prefer to borrow from their government rather than from private sources. For me, personally, to deny them or persuade the college to deny them the opportunity to make their own decisions would be an exercise of arbitrary power or a case of Big Brotherism. Both are evil." President Wilkinson said in a letter to the student committee: "This University for one, and I believe all the students in its student body, are proud to take an oath to support the Constitution of the United States."

The student committee exhorted pro-oath students to get their views before the public, and before Congress. Early in February, it issued the following instructions, offering a fair insight into the techniques of effective political advocacy:

Send us the names of other students, professors, or administrative officers of colleges and universities, who believe in keeping the loyalty oath clause in the National Defense Education Act. Speak to these people, and form a local Student Committee for the Loyalty Oath on your campus.

We are especially interested in getting the names of class officers, student body presidents, campus newspaper editors, political club officers, *and recipients of grants under the National Defense Education Act, who are sympathetic to our movement.*

Pass resolutions favorable to the loyalty oath in clubs and student organizations on your campus, and send the National Student Committee a copy of such resolutions.

Schedule debates on the loyalty oath, and arrange for pro-loyalty oath students to speak before community civic clubs, labor unions, business organizations, etc.

Display literature of the National Student Committee at student conventions and convocations on your campus.

Write letters to your campus newspaper, local community newspapers, and to your Senators and Congressmen. To obtain the names of your Senators and Congressmen, consult your political science department, or the community Democratic or Republican headquarters. *Individually-written letters are more effective than form letters, but student petitions are a good supplement to individual letters.*

This marshalling of sentiment was ·not lost on Washington. A steady stream of petitions and letters began to bombard the legislators.* Student lobbyists from the Committee's Washing-

---

* An amusing by-product of this effort was the experiment one oath-supporter conducted on Vice-President (then Senator) Lyndon John-

ton headquarters followed through with personal visits. Congress took heed.

"It is most heartening to me," said Republican Senator Styles Bridges of New Hampshire, "that an organization of the students themselves has come into being, dedicated to the preservation of the oath and disclaimer. Particularly heartening is the fact that membership comes from some of the colleges which have denied their students the freedom of choice."

Congressman Edgar Hiestand (R-Cal.) paid tribute to the group on the floor of the House. "Today," he said, "thousands of youths who are required to sign the oath are joining an organization which supports the provision as it is now written and administered. . . . This movement stems from the students themselves, rather than 'from the top down.'" Congressman Clarence Brown acclaimed the new group in a mailing to his constituents. Senator Spessard Holland (D-Fla.) also expressed his pleasure.

It was a new experience for these legislators: voices of agitation being raised, by young people, in behalf of conservatism. They had never seen anything like it.

The student committee did not confine itself to circulating petitions. Its leaders took on the formidable task of doing intellectual battle with the Griswolds and the Puseys—and did so with considerable effect. Their agitation brought them requests to speak before civic groups and to contribute articles to various senior publications; they seized the opportunity to charge that

---

son: writing Johnson two different letters, signed with different names, one in favor of the oath, one opposed to it. To the "pro" letter, Johnson answered: "As you may know, this question was before the Senate during the last session of Congress, and at that time I voted against removing this requirement as a condition to obtaining student loans under the act." To the "anti-" letter he replied: "I do not see that the disclaimer affidavit adds anything to the strength of the oath of allegiance required by the act."

the Griswold-Kennedy position was a denial, as Senator Bridges put it, of "freedom of choice."

In its first statement, the Loyalty Oath Committee had raised the questions: " (1) Whether it is proper for the officials of these colleges and universities that have refused participation to act as a super-legislature and deny qualified students the opportunity to seek the benefits under a public law designed to aid them individually, and (2) Whether such officials are not by administrative fiat depriving the students of the very freedom they seek to preserve."

Advocates of repeal were in an embarrassing position; they had taken a stance billed as a defense of persecuted students; yet that stance involved denying students the right of free choice, and the students were protesting loudly. "Not a single student in the United States," Doug Caddy told to a New York audience, "is being compelled to participate in the defense education program. The student's right to choose freely whether he will take the oath of undivided allegiance and participate in the program or not is his sacred American birthright. If his conscience or convictions forbid, he can choose not to."

As for the complaint of discrimination, the student committee observed that the N.D.E.A. participants were treated precisely as were other recipients of federal largess when the subsidized function was considered important to the "national defense."

In an address delivered in late February 1960, Caddy pointed out that similar oaths were required both of students in the ROTC and of students participating in the National Science Foundation Act of 1950:

According to the latest figures available from the Department of Defense, there are 155,871 college students enrolled in ROTC units across the nation during the current school year.

The number of ROTC students is more than twice as great as the total number of college students participating in the federal loan program—68,152 students as of November 1, 1959. Thus it would appear that for years ROTC students have been 'discriminated against' without their even knowing of it—since this fact was never brought to the attention of Congress. Still more pertinent is the fact that each year the Department of Defense awards hundreds of ROTC scholarships to prospective college students to subsidize their four years in college in an effort to develop career men (just as the N.D.E.A. is attempting to develop new leaders in certain fields).

In an article first printed in *The Individualist,* and reproduced widely in other publications, Dave Franke commented: "What would these critics have Congress do? Impose a loyalty oath on the entire population, in order to avoid discrimination? This certainly would come closer to a witch hunt than the present system. The argument defies all logic. . . . Persons who work for the federal government must take a loyalty oath. Should all citizens be required to an oath, to avoid ferreting out government employees as subjects for special distrust? The answer is obvious."

Moreover, it developed that, while President Griswold presumed to speak for the "colleges and universities," his backing in those quarters, although vociferous, was otherwise feeble. In his article, whenever he advanced an argument against the loyalty oath, Griswold referred to it as the position of the "colleges and universities." By my count this formulation appears in his article, in one way or another, no less than twenty-three times. That fact would be peculiar enough simply in the absence of proof that Griswold did speak, as he claimed, for America's "colleges and universities." It becomes all the more so when we consider that the "vast majority" of the colleges and universities, far from joining Yale and Harvard in their exodus from N.D.E.A., participated in the act without protest.

As of November 25, 1959, one week after Yale withdrew from the program, no less than 1,365 "colleges and universities" were participating in the N.D.E.A. Seventeen institutions had either withdrawn from the program, or had refused to participate in the first place; 12 others had participated under protest. If we subtract the 12 from the number of participating schools and add them in with the non-participants, we get 3,353 "colleges and universities" participating, 29 opposing—a ratio of about 45-to-1 in favor of the oath. The student committee saw to it that the true proportion did not go unnoticed by the public.

A final flourish of unreason—and indeed, the underlying fallacy of the whole campaign against the oath—drew the ire of the Loyalty Oath Committee. The act was passed, the students pointed out, as an instrument of "national defense." If the moneys disbursed under it were truly "defense" funds, how could it be argued that steps should not be taken to insure the loyalty of the recipients? "By what conceivable twist of logic," David Franke inquired, "can it be held that citizens who are loyal should be taxed to help an unloyal student through college as a defense measure?"

In its uproar against the oath and affidavit, the Liberal community raised some doubts about its sincerity in backing the N.D.E.A. in the first place. The bill had been advertised as a "defense" act, to capitalize on public consternation concerning Moscow's alleged advances in space. If the oath and affidavit were irrelevant, then the act could not really be an instrument of defense, and was passed under false pretenses; in which case, the answer was to repeal, not the loyalty oath, but the act itself. Arguments validating the act validate the oath; arguments invalidating the oath invalidate the act.*

* The two-way stretch of the Liberal mentality was well illustrated by the position taken on this point by Robert F. Goheen, President of

Slowly, the mood of Washington toward the "loyalty oath" had begun to change. Legislators were now uncomfortably aware that a considerable segment of the country—how considerable unknown, but enough in any event to provoke some second thoughts—opposed repeal. Proponents of S. 2929, observed columnist Holmes Alexander, "are matched, in fact, overmatched, by persons and institutions of the opposite viewpoint. A National Committee for the Loyalty Oath . . . has taken a Washington headquarters for the fight. It is an even bet that the 86th Congress (unless caught in a weak moment) will keep the law as it was written only two years ago."

The repeal forces managed to squeeze S. 2929 through the Senate—although the legislators prudently refrained from making a record vote on its passage. But that was the last gasp. The steam had gone out of the repeal drive, and, in the House, S. 2929 expired in committee. Though it would be challenged again another time, the loyalty oath had survived the first major onslaught.

"For a time," commented Republican Representative Frank Bow of Ohio, "it appeared to many of us that the requirement might be repealed. Senator Kennedy and others introduced bills to repeal the offending section of the law. . . . But something

---

Princeton University. "We object to the requirement of the loyalty affidavit and oath on principle," he said, "and because of deleterious effects we foresee from it. *At the same time we believe that federal aid to higher education, both public and private, is essential, and we believe that the new National Defense Education Act is, on the whole, a step in the right direction.* This forces us into a temporizing position. We are loath to see an emotional crisis generated over the loyalty oath, lest it jeopardize the possibility of enlarged appropriations for the N.D.E.A. which we believe to be so necessary." Which is about as close as one can come, without putting it in so many words, to confessing that those who want the act want it for reasons having nothing to do with national defense, but because they desire to see federal intervention in the educative process. [Italics are added.]

has cleared the air, and the repeal movement has lost momentum. That something is the good sense and patriotism of students who decided that there was nothing offensive about swearing allegiance to the United States of America." The agency which had saved the day, Bow surmised, was the National Student Committee for the Loyalty Oath. "I am happy," he concluded, "to see this revival of common sense and patriotism, and I hope it takes root and spreads."

Not all observers shared Bow's enthusiasm. The contentious Mr. Gerald Johnson threw a tantrum in the pages of the *New Republic*. This, he fumed, was *not* the way students were supposed to act. The readiness of young people to affirm their loyalty to their country was, in Johnson's view, "an outburst of servility." It simply proved these students were ignoramuses who could not think (irrespective of I.Q.), because they "have no conception of intellectual freedom"—as defined by Gerald Johnson. The fury of this attack, which made no attempt to grapple with the student committee's arguments, but simply bathed them in venom, was a dead giveaway. Mr. Johnson, a Liberal in his declining years, was nonplussed. He had seen the face of tomorrow, but he could not believe it.

In the upshot, Mr. Johnson's fulminations were to look increasingly dyspeptic, Representative Bow's hopeful forecast increasingly sound. In addition to its impact on the matter at hand, the student committee focused national attention on an unprecedented phenomenon: Students adopting an outspokenly conservative position on national issues—in rebellion against the Liberalism of their elders. It was a political turn which would gain considerable notoriety in the months ahead. And the band of young conservatives, the incipient structure of a national movement, remained intact. It would perform still other service in other battles.

V

Chicago, 1960

> "Senator Goldwater's frankness and dash won
> him a great victory in Arizona. . . . If he can in-
> fuse his principles and vigor into the Republi-
> cans, their party may display a liveliness it has
> not known since Theodore Roosevelt."
>
> RUSSELL KIRK

THE BATTLE OF THE LOYALTY OATH had been impor-
tant in many respects. It gave the young conservatives a taste of
political action—and even the sweet sensation of victory. And
it established a network of contacts which combined individual
strugglings into a single national endeavor. Students at work
on individual campuses became aware of others similarly engaged; face-to-face meetings, telephone conversations, frequent
correspondence bound them into something closer to a "movement," with a common idiom and common aspirations. They
had taken their first real step from philosophical speculation to
political action.

It was clear that action was what many of them wanted. In
the urgent categories of youth, they saw the world slipping
rapidly toward disaster. As their convictions had become more
settled—more a matter of affirmative belief than reaction

against the establishment—their feeling of alarm became more pronounced. That sense of urgency, inevitably, became translated into politics.

The conservative tendency of college students, as I have noted, was suggested by the heavy majorities received by Vice-President Nixon in straw polls taken during the 1960 campaign. It found an even sharper focus in the person of Senator Barry Goldwater, the outspoken Republican from Arizona. For Goldwater is the public official who speaks in the clear tones which mark the conservatism of the young—a fact which first gained recognition at the Republican Party's 1960 national convention. Ideological clarity, plus Goldwater's personal verve and energy, have drawn the rebellious young people to his standard.

Isolating the exact beginning of the Goldwater sentiment among young people is difficult. Enthusiasm for him has increased in proportion as the doctrines of conservatism have become diffused throughout the country, and it has emanated from many sources simultaneously. The circumstances under which this sentiment was crystallized and became formal, however, can be recorded. For the chain of events which led to the massive demonstration in Chicago had an identifiable beginning.

The movement began in Des Moines, Iowa, in April, 1960. The Midwest Federation of College Young Republican Clubs met there in a convention which developed into a bitter struggle between the forces of Liberal and conservative Republicanism. The meeting was something of a stand-off; the Liberal candidate for chairman squeezed through, by a margin of five votes, but the conservatives pushed over a surprise resolution of support for Goldwater—endorsing him for the vice-presidency. The resolution commended Goldwater for "outstanding service in defining and clarifying the sharp differences between the Republican and Democratic parties. . . ."

Among the delegates to that convention was a Northwestern University student named Robert Croll, shortly to become College Clubs Chairman of the Illinois Young Republicans. Struck by the enthusiastic response to Goldwater, Croll decided that the undertow of youthful conservatism was stronger than many people, including Croll himself, had suspected. A concerted effort to marshal young people to Goldwater's conservative banner might serve notice on the nation that American youth, as Croll put it, had "had their fill of government intervention, swollen bureaucracy, and the variety of 'internationalism' which holds that America can do no right, and her enemies can do no wrong. . . ." The Republican convention, barely three months away, offered a convenient focus for that kind of effort: a drive to put Goldwater on the Republican ticket.

Like other Young Republicans, Croll knew the Republican Presidential nomination was assured for Nixon, and had no inclination to challenge it. But the addition of Goldwater to the ticket, he felt, would provide a rallying point for conservatives and strengthen the Republican cause generally. He decided to begin agitation to gain Goldwater the Republican nomination for Vice-President.

Croll began calling a number of other conservative students, among them Doug Caddy and Dave Franke of the Loyalty Oath Committee, Robert Harley (President of the District of Columbia College Young Republicans), Richard Noble (Treasurer of the California Young Republicans) and John Weicher, a former staff member at *Human Events* and a student at the University of Chicago. These five became the executive committee of "Youth for Goldwater for Vice-President," which was unveiled for public inspection May 12, 1960—just a month after the Des Moines convention.

In his opening statement, Croll said: "There is no doubt in my mind that if Senator Goldwater were offered the GOP vice-presidential nomination he would accept it. Certainly there has been a far more extensive and intensive display of support by Republicans across the country for Senator Goldwater for that office than for any other possible candidate. The Senator is a proven vote-getter and in his capacity as head of the GOP Senatorial Campaign Committee has made many friends throughout the nation within the party who will work hard for him."

In support of his statement, Croll could cite not only the endorsement of the Midwest Federation, but a poll of Young Republicans by the Young Republican *News,* official publication of the Young Republican Federation, which showed Goldwater the number one choice (by a three to one margin) over the eventual nominee, Henry Cabot Lodge, for the vice-presidency.

The announcement of "Youth for Goldwater" did not cause a particular flurry at first. Apparently the wire services and newspapers did not take the idea seriously—that young people, whatever their feelings on the loyalty oath, could in fact rally to a figure so thoroughly conservative as Barry Goldwater. Yet in the short months between the launching of the group and the conclusion of the Republican convention, the idea came to be taken very seriously indeed.

In succeeding weeks, the Goldwater effort picked up numerous endorsements. The Young Republicans of Cook County, Illinois, the largest Young Republican group in the nation; the Republican Party of Wyoming; the Republican Party of Arizona, of Mississippi, and South Carolina; the Young Republicans of Idaho and Wisconsin, and the College Young Republicans of the District of Columbia—all came out for the Senator.

In a poll conducted by *Human Events,* Republican County Chairmen across the nation named Goldwater as their first choice for Vice President. And, most emphatic of all, the officials of "Youth for Nixon" in the Midwest met in Chicago and voted Goldwater their choice for the vice-presidency—by a margin of 14 to 2—over U.N. Ambassador Lodge.

As the endorsements accumulated, Youth for Goldwater quickened the pace of its organizational activities. Croll was flooded with requests for memberships in the organization—which for a dollar provided applicants with a copy of Goldwater's *Conscience of a Conservative,* bumper strips, Goldwater buttons, brochures, and literature quoting and extolling the Senator. Requests for charters from individual colleges and for whole states mounted rapidly. Beginning with a scatter of organizations in 12 states, by early July the group could announce "active Youth for Goldwater groups in 32 states and in the District of Columbia," with chapters representing 64 college and university campuses.

The leaders found themselves called upon by senior Republican and conservative groups for speeches on conservatism and statements on the progress of the campaign. At a meeting of the Chevy Chase Republican Women's Club in Maryland, Doug Caddy appeared to give an oral review of *The Conscience of a Conservative.* Goldwater, he said, offered "the American people a program by which they can restore many of the constitutional freedoms which have been lost." He added: "I expect that soon conservatism will be the 'thing to be.' "

When New York Governor Nelson Rockefeller delivered his famous repudiation of the Eisenhower administration, Youth for Goldwater immediately pounced on him. Chairman Croll denounced Rockefeller's assertion that the cold war could be prosecuted through increased government spending. He accused the New Yorker of "clouding issues and . . . giving aid and comfort to the very forces of weakness and confusion which have contributed so much to our series of retreats at the hands of the world Communist empire."

The Goldwater committee placed ads, announcing its progress and soliciting funds, in *The Wall Street Journal* and *National Review*. Their objectives, they announced, were " (1) to promote Senator Barry Goldwater as a candidate for the GOP vice-presidential nomination; (2) to work within the Young Republican National Federation for the political and economic philosophy expressed in Senator Goldwater's book, *The Conscience of a Conservative*." Again sounding the keynote of the conservative rebellion, the advertisement concluded: "For many years, conservatives have worried about the radicalism on our college campuses, and have hoped for a revival of youthful conservatism. We have arrived—but we need your support."

The surge of conservatism on the campus was daily becoming more apparent. "American youth," Croll declared in a speech July 21, "is swinging to the right—and swinging more rapidly all the time. Conservative activity was virtually non-existent ten years ago, was only mildly vigorous in 1955, and is going full speed now. I think the next ten years will see a full-scale triumph for conservative ideas in the decisive center of campus opinion."

In a fuller exposition of this view, Croll had delivered an address, part philosophical and part political, to a Youth for Goldwater rally in Chicago's LaSalle Hotel: "America's young conservatives today, as I have seen them, are united both by their enthusiasm in a common fight, and by their deep belief in the traditions and values of this nation. Thus, as its time approaches, as it is toughened and refined in the fires of crisis, conservatism grows always stronger, and must inevitably triumph."

Meanwhile, Youth for Goldwater chapters blossomed across the nation: in Ohio, in Texas, in Washington, in New York, in Missouri, in Vermont, in New Mexico, in Illinois, in Minnesota, in Georgia—even in Alaska.

At the Wisconsin GOP Republican convention, according to the *Press-Gazette* of Green Bay, "one of the hottest items was a big lapel button proclaiming the virtues of Sen. Barry Goldwater of Arizona for the presidential nomination of the GOP. Mrs. Ruth Murray of Oshkosh found such a demand that she started charging twenty-five cents apiece for the buttons." In Massachusetts, Jack Molesworth, a youthful member of the GOP State Committee, bolted to Goldwater for the vice-presidential nomination. An endorsement for Massachusetts' favorite son Henry Cabot Lodge, Molesworth charged, had been slipped through the GOP state convention. Molesworth was joined by Massachusetts publisher Basil Brewer, an old enemy of Lodge, who also endorsed Goldwater.

By convention time, the Goldwater phenomenon was too large to be ignored. "In a truly open convention Republicans would probably nominate Goldwater for Vice-President," said *Newsweek*. In Chicago, a consignment of Goldwater buttons, ten thousand in number, was gobbled up before proceedings even got under way. Even these rumblings, however, did not alert the public, or a number of Liberal pundits, to the full extent of the Goldwater sentiment—or to its youthful origins. Some Liberal columnists dismissed the boomlet as the "last gasp" of the Old Guard—the death rattle of an element that would soon be heard from no more. It took the convention itself to disabuse them of such notions.

Goldwater activity in Chicago was sporadic, disorganized, and thoroughly spontaneous. No less than four separate Goldwater committees—Americans for Goldwater, Goldwater for President, Youth for Goldwater, and a "Goldwater Coordinating Committee"—were on hand there, with headquarters in separate buildings. Most of the participants had come under their own steam, unaware that many others had also forged across the country with the same inspiration—to whoop it up for Barry Goldwater and, if possible, to win him a spot on the Republican ticket. His Arizona backers arrived in force, complete with a band of marching Indians. One contingent of conservatives came all the way from Houston, Texas, by bus. On the pre-convention week end of July 23-24, Goldwaterites poured into Chicago. And when the pols and the pundits got a look at them, some old estimates underwent a hasty revision.

"There is an impression abroad," wrote John Wyngaard in the Appleton, Wisconsin, *Post-Crescent,* "that the conservative bias in Republican politics is confined to the older politicians, the stalwarts of the pre-New Deal era. Yet it is an eye-catching fact that most of the paraders and flag-wavers in the Goldwater demonstration are young people."

That fact was indeed eye-catching, if that is the word for it, at Youth for Goldwater headquarters in the Columbia Room of the Pick-Congress. The room was a continual crush of young people, in quest of literature, signs, buttons, or one of the hundreds of yellow "Goldwater" balloons that clustered against the ceiling. The Goldwater leaders found themselves in the eye of a political hurricane, pumping out statements, maintaining a makeshift liaison with the other Goldwater groups and with Goldwater himself, answering questions and requests for help from the students who crowded the headquarters. Phones jangled, curious senior Republicans trooped in, reporters and photographers swarmed up the elevators to get a look at this new phenomenon.

These youngsters, of course, could wield little or no influence in the normal routine of political horse-trading; but they could issue a clear call for political principle, and they could make noise for their favorite—both of which they did. Everywhere in Chicago, in the streets and in the hotels, Goldwater signs bobbed above the crowds; young people wearing Goldwater buttons thronged the sidewalks; whenever the senator himself would appear, or some speaker would mention his name, a great cheer would go up.

The press increasingly paid heed, and carried the story to the nation. "This convention," wrote Vermont Royster in *The Wall Street Journal*, "is full of young delegates, and even younger followers, overrunning its corridors, who have lost the illusions of the generation before them about the wonders of the welfare state. . . . The young rebels of the 1930s, who toyed with socialism, are now the rebels against socialism's works."

The Cincinnati *Post-Times Star* took note of the senator's "loud, busy, serious and largely youthful corps of supporters."

In the *Philadelphia Bulletin,* Philip Schaefer observed that "if the pay-off was in the zeal of a man's supporters, instead of delegate votes, Senator Barry Goldwater of Arizona would be a shoo-in for the Republican presidential nomination. Or just about anything else out here. The 51-year-old ruggedly handsome hero of the Republican Party's conservative wing has stirred up particular enthusiasm among young people. . . ."

The Goldwater push, said the *Post-Standard* of Syracuse, "has been ripening for several years on the vines of a growing trend to conservatism, similar to the splurge of liberalism in the 1930s, on campuses across the nation. The Republican National Convention is currently spotlighting this trend."

On Sunday evening, July 24, a huge Goldwater rally was held in the Morrison Hotel.* The Goldwater for President committee paraded a mass of petitions containing fifty thousand signatures, urging Goldwater for the presidency. The room was packed with one thousand cheering Goldwaterites, many of them young people. Former Senator William E. Jenner of Indiana addressed the group, surveyed the room, and remarked that today's youngsters "had a damn sight more sense than their mommies and daddies." "That rally," he later told a reporter, "was about the most lively affair so far. I was impressed by the number of young people who are for Goldwater. They will be conservatives—if our ideas are properly presented to them."

And, the following day, I heard a still more authoritative commentary—from a Chicago taxi-driver. Chauffeuring me from the Palmer House to the Blackstone, the cabby noticed my typewriter.

"You up here to cover the convention?"

"Yes," I said.

"Want to know who the people at this convention *really* like?"

"Who do they like?"

"This guy Goldwater," he said. "Everywhere you go, you see those huge pictures of him—look, there's a couple over there. And people are always getting in my cab and giving me Goldwater literature." He held up a wad of it. "Like some?"

"No thanks," I said, "I have plenty; but tell me, what do you think of Goldwater?"

"I don't know much about politics," he said. "But I saw this guy on television last night, and I think he's got something. I mean he *stands* for something, if you get me."

---

* Staged by New Orleans publishers and conservative activists Kent and Phoebe Courtney.

I "got" what the cabby meant, all right—and as the Gold-water surge pounded forward, a lot of other people got it, too.

The Liberals were baffled. They grasped for analogies, for some formula that would explain this burst of conservatism. Nothing seemed to work. One newspaper compared the Gold-water boom to "the one that hoisted Adlai Stevenson to idolatry among some Democrats." But, as columnist Ralph de Toledano observed, the Stevenson effort was disciplined, the Goldwater effusion was spontaneous. And there was the real story. For behind the spontaneity was the deep conviction of youngsters who had grasped the intellectual message of conservatism, and who were articulate in conveying it. This seemed to be the most surprising aspect of the Goldwater movement. Youth for Gold-water GHQ, reported Russell Baker in *The New York Times,* was "manned by a group of young campus intellectuals." Rich-ard Stout of the *Chicago Daily News* quoted Bob Croll as say-ing Goldwater possessed "charismatic appeal," dourly explain-ing that "charismatic is an egghead word describing someone with a special divine or spiritual gift or endowment fitting him for an office to which called, according to Webster's unabridged dictionary." Schaefer of the *Bulletin* noted that "the Goldwater gang is mostly collegiate, articulate, and convinced right-wingers who'd sooner discuss constitutional Republicanism than hand you one of their yellow-and-blue balloons."

As the tides of the convention shifted back and forth, the articulate young conservatives gained considerable publicity for the facts (a) that there was strong sentiment in the GOP for fidelity to conservative principles, and (b) that the dele-gates, given a free choice, would unquestionably have put Gold-water on the ticket. Both facts had been suggested when Goldwater appeared before the platform committee, to state his views on Republican philosophy. In contrast to Nelson

Rockefeller, who was received with stiff courtesy, Goldwater
was greeted with a vigorous ovation. He received another on
the opening night of the convention, when he was called upon
to speak in behalf of 1960's GOP candidates for the Senate. His
appearance touched off a burst of adulation that was gavelled
from the aisles after eight minutes of political delirium.

The young conservatives, commented de Toledano, "were set
up by the demonstration Mr. Goldwater received from the
floor, and by the fact that the Republican National Committee
had allowed him to address the convention. Originally, Senator Goldwater had been told that he would not be included
among the speakers. A flood of several thousand telegrams, protesting bitterly against this 'discrimination,' led to a change in
plans."

That same evening, the pressure had been turned on to "Liberalize" the party platform. Nixon and Rockefeller were working in tandem to jam through a strong "civil rights" plank,
to the dismay of the platform committee conservatives. Additionally, word filtered through the convention that Henry
Cabot Lodge, Ambassador to the United Nations and certified
Back Bay Liberal, would be tapped as Nixon's running mate.
Dick Noble of Stanford, Western Vice-Chairman of the Committee, issued a blistering statement. "The big question of this
convention," he said, "and the unanswered one, is whether the
fight for the vice-presidency nomination is going to be an open
one or whether it is going to be decided in the back rooms." On
the basis of pre-convention commitments and the widespread
rumblings of dissent in Chicago, Noble claimed, 325 delegates
were in Goldwater's pocket for the second spot. "Talk around
the hotel lobbies of the convention," he added, "appears to
show that there are many other . . . delegates just waiting for
the chance to pledge themselves for Goldwater."

Noble's boast was more than campaign rhetoric. With the mounting pressures for "Liberalization," senior Republicans had begun to reflect the contagious enthusiasm of the young. Chafing under the compact struck by Nixon and Rockefeller, a number of delegations wavered toward Goldwater—not for Vice President, but for President. Goldwater himself had stiffened against the idea of his name being put up for the second position. "I'm afraid I might get it," he told a group of his young followers at the Pick-Congress.

As the "civil rights" battle raged, delegates grumbled and cursed at the pressures from "upstairs." In the teeming corridors and jammed elevators of the Palmer House, admiration for Goldwater was expressed freely and often. In more than one caucus, angry men arose to denounce the Liberal trend of the convention.

By Tuesday morning, July 26, the Goldwater uprising was strong enough for reporters to start counting votes. The Arizona senator had come to town with presidential pledges from his home state and from South Carolina. Wyoming, Mississippi and Texas were committed to him for the vice-presidency, and the last two were on the verge of recaucusing to move that commitment up a notch. The deepest rumblings were in the disaffected South. Louisiana endorsed Goldwater for the number-one spot. There were noises of apostasy in Virginia and Georgia. Outside the South, Goldwater-for-President murmurs were emanating from South Dakota and Nevada.

None of it, of course, was enough to suggest that Goldwater could make even a medium-sized dent in Nixon's assured majority. But it was enough to indicate that a Goldwater nomination would be the occasion for a symbolic affirmation of conservative spirit, and to encourage the Goldwaterites to make the try. The Goldwater strategists decided to enter the Senator as a nominee for President. The crucial question became—how impressive, or unimpressive, would the affirmation be?

Word came down that the Senator was going to be nominated, and the young conservatives went to work to prepare a demonstration for him. Posters were nailed to sticks. Two workers were dispatched to buy all the confetti and all the parade streamers they could locate. "Goldwater" balloons were inflated by the thousands. The band of marching Indians was alerted. Demonstrators were briefed on staging points and cheers.

Then, on Wednesday night, July 27, the name of Nixon was placed before the convention. A massive demonstration, beautifully orchestrated, swept over the hall, and continued for approximately twenty minutes. The young Goldwater backers were apprehensive. I stood on the convention floor next to two of them as they engaged in nervous conversation. "We better call it off," said one. "We can't match this. Our demonstration is going to look sick." "We can't call it off now," said the other. "Go get your people ready."

The Nixon demonstration ended, and in that packed and sweltering hall, Governor Paul Fannin of Arizona strode to the podium. He was going to nominate Goldwater for the highest honor the United States can bestow.

The Goldwaterites tensed. Had they labored frantically for months, and then through these hectic days of the convention, to have their effort collapse at last in humiliation and failure? They scattered about the convention floor, urging their colleagues to be at the ready. As feeble as the demonstration might be, they were going to give it their all.

Fannin's flowery speech rolled on. At the two rear entrances to the Stockyards, a horde of Goldwater sympathizers with banners, posters, horns and other paraphernalia of a demonstration strained to get inside. One observer estimated the total number at three thousand.

Fannin's speech ended: ". . . for President of the United States, Senator Barry Goldwater of Arizona." The words swept through the auditorium, and were suddenly lost in bedlam. A great wave of sound exploded into the vaulted reaches of the stockyards. The demonstrators charged through the rear entrances. Delegates leaped to their feet. State signs bobbed in the aisles: Louisiana, Georgia, South Dakota, Wyoming, Texas, Indiana, Colorado, even Massachusetts. The Indians marched, delegates poured into the aisles, more demonstrators struggled to get into the Amphitheater.

I had been standing in an aisle holding my breath. Surrounded by a melee of shouting humanity, I could see nothing. I fought my way back to the pressbox, clambered up onto a table, and looked out over the swirling demonstration.

At the back of the platform, Goldwater appeared. He stepped forward to Representative Halleck, Chairman of the Convention, and said: "May I say a few words?" A great roar shook the hall, as the entire convention came to its feet. The volley of sound doubled—and redoubled. The ovation for the outspoken senator, for the courage of his views, was real and deep, and it was overwhelming. It packed the stockyards with emotions that had been pent and confined through five days of intense leftward pressure. Then, with the nation watching, Goldwater made his famous speech, withdrawing his name from contention.

The demonstration, by any standard, was a stunning success. But the Young Goldwaterites felt it could have been even better, if the convention officials had let it. A vehement complaint about the handling of the demonstration was lodged by one

Youth for Goldwater official, James T. Kolbe of Patagonia, Arizona. In a letter mailed to newspapers around the country, Kolbe said:

As one who participated in the recent effort to secure a place for Senator Barry Goldwater on the national Republican ticket, I feel it is imperative to call attention to certain inequities which marked the handling of candidates' demonstrations at the Republican convention.

Innumerable young people and other volunteers worked long and hard in behalf of Senator Goldwater's candidacy, and many travelled hundreds and even thousands of miles to contribute their time and their energies.

What happened to them when they reached the culmination of their efforts was a shocking disillusionment with the political methods resorted to by some of their elders. These young volunteers found themselves confronted with what was clearly an attempt to deny them equal opportunity to make their feelings known.

The peak of the Goldwater effort, owing to the circumstances of the convention, was to be a demonstration for the Senator Wednesday evening, July 27. It was learned only that day that Governor Paul Fannin of Arizona would submit Senator Goldwater's name as a candidate for President. The various Goldwater volunteers then tried to arrange for a suitable demonstration, and thousands of loyal Goldwater backers appeared at the Chicago Amphitheater to participate.

What happened that evening can be described only as an open violation of the elementary requirements of fair play. Vice-President Nixon was the beneficiary of a suitably robust demonstration which lasted for 18 minutes, and in which close to 2,500 outside demonstrators were herded into the hall, the convention band played constantly at top volume, and the cheering delegates were allowed to march across the center aisles of the arena. It was a fitting tribute to the Vice-President, and we object to none of it. But we do object vigorously to the unequal treatment accorded those who wanted to demonstrate for Senator Goldwater—as follows:

1. The great bulk of his demonstrators, many of whom had travelled from the remote corners of America at considerable

personal expense, were not allowed on to the convention floor. A cordon of armed guards prevented them from getting in the gates, at some times resorting to physical violence. A fair estimate would be that less than one half of the 250 people with Goldwater demonstrator passes were allowed on the floor, while the Nixon demonstrators were permitted to flood the hall regardless of whether or not they had passes.

2. The demonstrators who were allowed in were forced to march directly down the side aisles and then out. Since they were largely hidden behind the rows of standing delegates, it is doubtful whether many of them were seen at all.

3. Even delegates on the floor were not permitted to demonstrate in the lateral aisles which intersected the line of sight of the television cameras. The aisles at the front and the back of the auditorium were completely blocked off to everyone, delegate or otherwise, who was holding a Goldwater sign. Since these aisles were at that time relatively empty, and since they had been used freely during the Nixon demonstration, it is obvious the intent of those in charge was to keep as much of the demonstration as possible from the sight of the television viewers.

4. The convention orchestra, which played at pain-point intensity throughout the Nixon demonstration, could barely be heard during the demonstration for Senator Goldwater. While it kept up for the full 18 minutes for Nixon, it played for less than five during the effort for Goldwater.

What all this adds up to should be clear on the face of it. It is an overwhelming tribute to Senator Goldwater, and to his determined stand for traditional Republicanism, that the demonstration in his behalf was nevertheless prolonged and enthusiastic. This letter is to let your readers know that, had it not been for the actions of the convention authorities, what appeared on the nation's television screens would have been an even more stunning expression of loyalty to Goldwater and his principled conservatism.

The net result of the convention was to move the entire spectrum of Republican politics to the right. Prior to Chicago, the poles of GOP ideology were supposed to be Nixon on the right, Rockefeller on the left. Goldwater was thought to be an oddity, off by himself in the corner. When the smoke cleared, it was Rockefeller who was the oddity, and Goldwater who represented the "alternative" to Nixon.

Before the convention the press was laden with speculation about Rockefeller, his intentions, and his supposed magnetism. Once things got under way, it became painfully apparent that the "draft Rockefeller" movement was synthetic, a balloon inflated with money. Repeatedly, reporters noted the lavish expenditure of the Rockefeller forces, and the youthful, if penurious, zeal of the Goldwater camp. Commenting on a Young Republican parade, the Washington *Star* said: "The Youth for Goldwater movement almost took over the parade with its caravan of tooting cars and cheering youngsters. The prize for sheer opulence should go, however, to the colorful ship float that carried a bevy of draft-Rockefeller girls." Peter Edson described the Youth for Goldwater movement as a "shoestring operation."

The Detroit *News* observed that the Rockefeller contingent was distrusted by the majority of the convention, the Nixon-for-President backers, but that the Goldwater forces were not. "It's common," write J. F. Ter Horst, "to find a person with a flamboyant blue and gold 'Americans for Goldwater' badge talking easily with an 'I'm for Nixon' Republican in convention headquarters at the Conrad Hilton Hotel. But the average Nixon booster acts mighty uncomfortable when stopped by one of Gov. Nelson A. Rockefeller's bemedalled backers."

William V. Shannon of the New York *Post* (hardly a friendly observer) summed it up: "Goldwater was truly the hero of the convention." Shannon added:

He appeared before the platform Committee and as he made his recommendations, he was greeted with wave after wave of applause. He addressed the convention twice and both times received genuinely fervent ovations. His press conferences drew a big turnout of reporters. The sidewalks and hotel lobbies were repeatedly jammed with platoons of 'Youth for Goldwater' demonstrators.

Nixon, in his acceptance speech Thursday night, linked the names of Goldwater and Rockefeller in the same paragraph, assigning them, in effect, equal status as figures in the party. No one doubted that Nixon had not dared permit a make-believe 'open convention' decision on the Vice Presidency with the delegates choosing from a list of approved candidates. If the delegates had been permitted even this limited freedom, they might very well have stampeded to Goldwater.

It was in all respects a remarkable achievement for Goldwater. By his skillful handling of himself in the past 10 days, he has established himself as the successor to the late Sen. Taft as leader and popular idol of the conservative Old Guard of the Republican party. He has successfully negotiated that difficult leap from being merely a state or regional politician to being a major national figure.

That convention, and that demonstration, made Barry Goldwater a famous man in America. Millions of people who had heard of him only vaguely or not at all were exposed to his philosophy, saw the explosion of genuine sentiment for him, and heard him speak eloquently of conservatism and the future of the Republican Party.

And, as it put Goldwater on the map, the demonstration put young conservatism on the map. From that time forward, reporters, commentators, and pundits became acutely aware of the rise of conservative sentiment among the young.

Since that time, Goldwater himself has become an evangelist propounding the good news of youthful conservatism. And his own following among college students has swollen into a massive national phenonemon.

"One of the reasons there is a swing back toward conservatism," he says, "must be in the rebellious nature of youth. I can remember during my own years in college in the late twenties, that at that time they were beginning to rebel against conservatism, which was the political order of the day." "Young people," he adds, "reason rightly that if Liberalism, or radicalism as they are growing to call it, has not produced the answer in the last thirty years or so to the same problems that existed when Roosevelt came in, then there must be some other means of approaching them. And conservatism might be that instrument."

Goldwater also observes: "Conservative political philosophy is an ancient faith, but it still speaks vigorously to the problems of today, and the undeniable truth of the conservative position is now attracting the enthusiastic loyalty of thousands of young people . . . in my visits to colleges, and even to grammar schools and high schools, I have always found an understanding and an enthusiasm among the students to strengthen my contention that conservatism will very probably be the wave of the future."

During the school year 1960-61, Goldwater spoke to fifty-five college groups. He had sixty-five college speaking engagements scheduled for 1961-62. Charles Lucey of Scripps-Howard gives a sample of Goldwater's continuing campaign to carry the message of conservatism to the campus. "This Taft-with-glamor," Lucey wrote last spring, "buzzed into town recently from a swing west to Arizona, California, and way points. He flew to the West again to address a joint session of the Iowa legislature and then on to Los Angeles for another college campus meeting. His travels after Easter continued the pace. Rose Polytechnic Institute in Indiana, Grinnell College in Iowa, Holy Cross at Worcester, Mass., two meetings at Harvard, one at Boston College, Princeton, Vassar, Hunter College in New York. Already he has four commencements ahead—at Brigham Young in Utah, Hamilton College in New York, Ari-

zona State University, and Asheville School at Asheville, N. C."
And so it goes.

The efforts of Youth for Goldwater paid off, in gold chips.
What had begun as a sudden inspiration at a college convention in Des Moines had blossomed into an authentic movement,
and finally into one of the outstanding facts of political life
in America—a fact which few forecasters could leave out of their
presidential figuring for 1964.

VI

Young Americans for Freedom

> "The preponderant judgment of the American people, especially the young people, is that the radical, or Liberal, approach has not worked and is not working. They yearn for a return to conservative principles."
>
> SENATOR BARRY GOLDWATER

IT WAS A BLISTERING CHICAGO AFTERNOON in late July. Street cleaners swept away the litter along Michigan Boulevard and hotel employees set about reordering the dishevelled wake of the departing delegates. The Republican convention had come and gone. But some of the participants remained.

Gathered in the Columbia Room of the Pick-Congress were the executive committee of the Youth for Goldwater drive, and a half-dozen other young conservatives. In the consummation of the Goldwater effort, a powerful force had been brought into being. But no one was sure what would happen next. Would the elements fused in the Chicago crucible dissolve and recede to their various campuses and regions? Or could the energy of the campaign be sustained, channeled into further organized activity? Determined not to let the conservative momentum die, the young conservatives resolved upon a new organization. They would issue a call for a national conference of young conservatives, early in the fall, to hammer out the details. An interim committee was established, under the direction of Doug Caddy, to contact the youth leaders and to make physical arrangements.

Accordingly, on the weekend of September 9-11, 1960, more than one hundred young conservatives, representing forty-four colleges, assembled in Sharon, Connecticut, at the family home of William F. Buckley, Jr. In two days, after the usual quota of parliamentary wrangling, the conference emerged with a new organization called "Young Americans for Freedom" (address: 79 Madison Ave., New York City). Its national chairman was Robert Schuchman of Yale Law School—an alumnus of the conservative group which had emerged from the Bronx High School of Science; Caddy was chosen as National Director.

The new group leaned heavily for leadership on active members of the national Young Republicans. Regional Chairmen included Robert Harley of Georgetown University, then Chairman of the District of Columbia College YRs; George Gaines, Chairman of Louisiana Youth for Nixon; Dick Noble, Treasurer of the California YRs; Bob Croll, Illinois collegiate YR chairman and leader of the Youth for Goldwater drive; and James Kolbe, Chairman of Arizona Youth for Goldwater.

The same element was represented in the Board of Directors: David Franke, Editor of the *Campus Republican;* James Abstine, then Chairman of the Indiana College Young Republicans, later elected a regional officer of the collegiate YRs; Howard Phillips, Chairman, Massachusetts Youth for Nixon (and President of the Harvard Student Council); Lee Edwards, Editor of the Young Republican *News* and press aide to Senator John Marshall Butler of Maryland; Carol Bauman, executive secretary of College Youth for Nixon; and Diarmuid

O'Scannlain, Foreign Affairs Chairman of the Young Republican National Federation. (Other YRs have been active at the
state level; e.g., Arthur McGonigle, Jr., Florida YAF chairman,
has also been state chairman of the college Young GOP and
Youth for Nixon organizations.)

The directors also included Richard Cowan of Yale; Tom
Colvin of Davidson College; William Madden of Holy Cross;
William Schulz of Antioch; Scott Stanley, Jr., of the University
of Kansas Law School; Herbert Kohler, Jr., of Knox College;
and Carl T. McIntire of Shelton College.

The purpose of YAF, as set forward in its first statement to
the press, was to "mobilize support among American youth for
conservative political candidates and legislation and to act as
spokesmen for conservative opinion on key issues affecting
young people."

Chairman Schuchman declared that "the tremendous growth
of conservative sentiment among the youth of the country cul-
minated in the meeting held in Sharon this last weekend. We
believe an organized and dedicated conservative youth can materially affect the course of political events and help America
attain the free society envisioned by its founders."

To define that free society, as they believed the founders had
envisioned it, the delegates had adopted the following statement:

In this time of moral and political crisis, it is the responsibility of the youth of America to affirm certain eternal truths.
We, as young conservatives, believe:
That the foremost among the transcendent values is the individual's use of his God-given free will, whence derives his right
to be free from the restrictions of arbitrary force;
That liberty is indivisible, and that political freedom cannot long exist without economic freedom;
That the purposes of government are to protect these free-

doms through the preservation of internal order, the provision of national defense, and the administration of justice;

That when government ventures beyond these rightful functions, it accumulates power which tends to diminish order and liberty;

That the Constitution of the United States is the best arrangement yet devised for empowering government to fulfill its proper role, while restraining it from the concentration and abuse of power;

That the genius of the Constitution—the division of powers —is summed up in the clause which reserves primacy to the several states, or to the people, in those spheres not specifically delegated to the federal government;

That the market economy, allocating resources by the free play of supply and demand, is the single economic system compatible with the requirements of personal freedom and constitutional government, and that it is at the same time the most productive supplier of human needs.

That when government interferes with the work of the market economy, it tends to reduce the moral and physical strength of the nation; that when it takes from one man to bestow on another, it diminishes the incentive of the first, the integrity of the second, and the moral autonomy of both;

That we will be free only so long as the national sovereignty of the United States is secure; that history shows periods of freedom are rare, and can exist only when free citizens concertedly defend their rights against all enemies;

That the forces of international Communism are, at present, the greatest single threat to these liberties;

That the United States should stress victory over, rather than co-existence with, this menace; and

That American foreign policy must be judged by this criterion: does it serve the just interests of the United States?

This manifesto became known as "the Sharon Statement"— a charter of principles by which to judge political issues, upon which to premise political action. How the principles would apply, in practical circumstances, remained to be seen. A crucial test case was soon to emerge, short weeks after the founding

conference. A number of the founders were Young Republicans; a presidential campaign was in progress, and they were
working hard in behalf of the Republican candidate, Richard
Nixon. The question arose: Should YAF issue an endorsement
of Nixon? Or should it stay out of the campaign? After deep
consideration, the leaders decided against an endorsement.

That decision has touched off some barbed comment by
YAF's Liberal opposition. The refusal, it was alleged, was a
Machiavellian stroke aimed at exonerating the YAF leaders
from Nixon's defeat. A Liberal youth publication called *Advance* charged that "YAF can now cry 'I told you so,' and plump
for Goldwater in '64." *Advance,* be it noted, is an unblushing
house organ of Rockefeller modernism; its editors may thus be
too quick to think in terms of the distant calculations sometimes imputed to their own leader, whose state piled up robust
majorities against Nixon in the 1960 election. Its allegation,
in any event, ignores the fact that YAF's leadership included
not only the national executive secretary of College Youth for
Nixon, but two state Youth of Nixon chairmen, and no less
than eight other people serving, in one capacity or another, as
Young Republican officials; and that, in those identities, each
was bending every effort to help achieve Nixon's election.

Advance itself noted that Goldwater had been the first to
proclaim "I told you so" when Nixon lost; yet Goldwater *had*
endorsed Nixon, in addition to stumping the country for him.
Obviously, there is nothing about an endorsement prior to an
election which precludes Monday-morning quarterbacking
after it. And, had Nixon won, an endorsement might have
stood YAF in good stead at the White House. Why, then, was
it withheld?

The answer is that YAF's decision had very little to do with
the immediate crisis in Republican politics, and everything to

do with the future of YAF. Its leaders, in reaching their decision, had reasoned roughly as follows: An endorsement by an infant organiaztion would do Nixon very little good; those who wanted his election could best achieve it—not by issuing statements in the name of a weeks-old youth group—but by going home and working in the precincts; and most of the YAF people were doing just that.

But while an endorsement could not materially help Nixon, it might have done a great deal of harm to YAF; principally, it would have established the group as a appendage of the Republican Party. Since YAF was formed to promote, not the Republican Party per se, but conservatism, an endorsement would have altered its principle function at the outset. There was, after all, a youth group already in operation devoted to advancing the GOP cause as such—the Young Republican National Federation, with its various constituent organizations. Why, the conservative leaders reasoned, erect a new organization merely to duplicate the function of the YRs?

The same reasoning covered the argument that, since Nixon was the more conservative of the two candidates, YAF would be advancing conservatism by endorsing him. Would not the Republican candidate, in almost any election in the North, be relatively more conservative than the Democrat? And wouldn't it follow that YAF would, by this argument, be constrained to endorse *every* Republican—including Rockefeller, or Case, or Javits? And wouldn't this, in turn, reduce the group to the status of a secondary Young Republican organization?

The alternative, it was decided, was to reserve endorsements for candidates whose views explicitly coincided with the Sharon Statement, rather than appeared as simply "more conservative" than their opposition. Thus it was determined the YAF, in spite of its heavy representation from Young Republican circles,

was not to be a "Republican" group. That initial decision on
the Nixon matter was crucial; for it established the organization as authentically nonpartisan, and authentically dedicated
to the advancement of conservatism, irrespective of party labels.

With that fundamental determination made, YAF launched
an extensive organizational effort. Its regional chairmen went
to work recruiting members, and the national office threw itself
into the ideological crises of the moment. A major Liberal-conservative struggle in the latter months of 1960 concerned the
House Committee on Un-American Activities. A considerable
campaign had been launched by the forces of the left, aimed
at either abolishing the committee or cutting back its appropriation. The campaign was to crescendo January 2, 1961—the
day the 87th Congress convened. Notably active in this effort,
at the far left end of the spectrum, was the "youth contingent"
of the Communist Party. Led by two youth agitators identified
under oath as Communists, a group of anti-HUAC demonstrators were to assemble in Washington the day Congress opened.
Their purpose: To buttonhole congressmen, to picket the
White House, and to stage a mass rally at the Capital's All Souls
Unitarian Church. The sponsors hoped to create the impression
that "youth" opposed the House Committee, and thus generate
emotional backing for its abolition.

Alerted to this plan, Young Americans for Freedom resolved
upon a counter-demonstration. Its leaders arranged for several
busloads of anti-Communist young people to travel from New
York to Washington. Similar delegations, marshalled from
other states and from other patriotic groups, converged on the
Capital. In all, better than four hundred pro-HUAC demonstrators were assembled to oppose the "abolitionist" effort.

The rival groups turned out, January 2, to demonstrate in
Lafayette Park, across the street from the White House. The

result, as one reporter phrased it: "A leftist march on Washington billed as a student demonstration against the House Committee on Un-American Activities collided today in front of the White House with a larger group of Committee supporters . . . *For the first time in the memory of veteran observers of such exhibitions, anti-Communists outnumbered those demanding abolition of the House committee, more than two-to-one. . . .*

"The largest rival group was Young Americans for Freedom, 150 in number, all of college age, headed by a Manhattan college senior, Dennis Brennen. They also had travelled by bus from New York City after reading of the planned demonstrations."

The net effect was to turn the tables on the radical left. Historically, the use of picket-line techniques, to dramatize one's case, to generate public sympathy, and to obtain newspaper publicity, has been almost exclusively a Liberal property. Manning a picket-line is not congenial to conservative temperament; even the most dedicated conservative has preferred the role of the contemplative, weighing and analyzing events from a distance. At the January 2 demonstration and counter-demonstration, all this was reversed. Conservatives had finally grasped the key importance of such displays—their impact on the public mind. For a pedestrian passing a picket line, or a newspaper reader seeing a picture of one, will generally conclude that if some people feel *this* strongly about an issue, there must be a lot more of the same general persuasion.

Thanks in part to this effort, the energy went out of the "abolition" drive. Congressman James Roosevelt, champion of the anti-Committee forces in the House, had already abandoned ship. HUAC's enemies were thoroughly deflated; pro-Committee sentiment had carried the day. When HUAC's appropriation at last came to a vote, it passed by a margin of 412-6.

The left had found itself beaten with its own favorite technique—a profoundly demoralizing experience. Only 212 abolitionist pickets turned up, although previous estimates and predictions had ranged from 500 to 2,000. "Their evening meeting," said one pro-HUAC demonstrator, "looked more like a funeral than a rally. Some listened apathetically and others slept while Burton White, Aubrey Williams and Dr. Willard Uphaus went through their regular scripts. The evening's activities ended as the picketers filed silently into their buses. The air was filled not with the radical-labor songs they usually sing, but with the resounding chants of the anti-Communist pickets that surrounded their buses."

This young conservative adds: "An important aspect of the affair is the fact that this was the first experience of Young Americans for Freedom in organizing a picket line; and they planned it for only two weeks, whereas the radical left had been planning its demonstrations for months, and had years of experience. A policeman remarked that 'this is the first time we've seen anything like this—where the anti-Communists are in the majority.' The policemen were among the first to experience the subtle change occurring in the country; the passing of the initiative in political propaganda from the youth of the left to the youth of the right."

Its appetite for combat whetted by this experience, YAF forged on with the fight in behalf of HUAC. With typical audacity, the group staged a showing of the HUAC documentary, "Operation Abolition," in Greenwich Village—the traditional heartland of American radicalism.

The Greater New York Council of YAF, led by Dave Franke, Rosemary McGrath, Clendenin Ryan and Myrna Bain, also organized its first local Chapter in Greenwich Village. The club was established in the Village purposely, says Franke, "to let the Liberals and those to their left know that no bastion is safe for them anymore." From the success of the YAF film showing there, written up most respectfully in the *Village Voice*, the message should have carried home. And if the Village is vulnerable, what fastness *is* safe for American Liberalism?

The New York Council, in its hectic round of activities, suggests what the organization hopes to accomplish throughout the country. The New York group issues its own bi-weekly bulletin, edited by Doris Sukop, to keep members posted on conservative activities of the moment. As of this writing, the publication goes to one thousand readers; as YAF's organizing efforts continue, its circulation should increase geometrically.*

The effort to articulate the organization into subunits is testimony to YAF's serious political intentions. The emphasis of the New York group "is on political action at the neigh-

---

* A typical issue (for January 23, 1961) contains the following announcements: a forthcoming "Freedom Forum," sponsored by the Citizens Anti-Communist Committee, in Bridgeport, Conn., featuring talks by Fulton Lewis III, Howard Kershner (Editor of *Christian Economics*), and C. H. Lowe, Counsellor at the Embassy of the Republic of China; a TV debate between Republican Congressman Walter Judd of Minnesota and Hugh Gaitskell, head of Britain's Labor Party; a commemoration of Freedom Day (when 22,000 Chinese and North Koreans refused to return to their Communist homelands), sponsored by the Assembly of Captive European Nations; an address by a YAF officer to the American Legion; a showing of "Operation Abolition" at Sarah Lawrence College, with commentary by Fulton Lewis III; a radio appearance by author-editor Frank Meyer; speeches by Walter Judd and Senator Barry Goldwater; a debate betweeen William F. Buckley, Jr. and Charles Taft; a National Review Forum, featuring George Sokolsky, Eugene Lyons, and Henry Hazlitt; a speech by Democratic Senator Thomas Dodd of Connecticut, at the monthly meeting of New York YAF; a speech by Goldwater in Perth Amboy; and plugs for radio broadcasts by Fulton Lewis, Jr. and Clarence Manion.

borhood level. . . . These clubs will sponsor speakers in their neighborhoods, social affairs, lectures, debates. Their members will be given instructions in the ABCs of local political action —petition drives, primary contests, election laws and regulations, distribution of campaign literature, doorbell ringing."

The ultimate object is to see men in office congenial to the aspirations of the Sharon Statement. "Sometimes our YAF chapters will find their own candidates for office," Franke says. "More often, however, their support will be given to those persons, already in office or announced as candidates, who are proven to be conservative and anti-Communist."

In addition to its grass-roots effort, YAF has successfully ventilated conservative opinion at the national level. One of its newest, and most impressive, ventures is the publication of a magazine called *The New Guard*. Its first issue featured an article on HUAC, a profile of conservative young Republican Congressman John Rousselot of California, a critique of the Liberal press, a column of Washington commentary, and a clutch of lively film and book reviews.

In its opening editorial statement, *The New Guard* sounded what is by now the familiar keynote of the new conservatives:

"Ten years ago this magazine would not have been possible. Twenty years ago it would not have been dreamed of. Thirty-five years ago it would not have been necessary. Today, *The New Guard* is possible, it is a reality, and it is needed by the youth of America to proclaim loudly and clearly: We are sick unto death of collectivism, socialism, statism and the other utopian isms which have poisoned the minds, weakened the wills and smothered the spirits of Americans for three decades and more."

The rhetoric is, perhaps, a trifle aggressive—but withal in keeping with the spirit of the organization. For YAF, as Bill

Buckley has noted, is marked by its "appetite for power," and for action. It clearly does not mean to abate its activities until the last vestiges of Liberalism have been removed from our government. And who is to say that job is as impossible as once it seemed?

As the Greenwich Village meeting suggests, one of YAF's principal endeavors has been to show the motion picture, "Operation Abolition," depicting the Communist-led San Francisco riots of May, 1960, and to provide speakers capable of dismantling the various Liberal allegations mounted against it. In turn, the film itself has been a powerful influence for awakening young people to the dangers of Communism. Fulton Lewis III, the film's 25-year-old narrator who has made several presentations of "Operation Abolition" under YAF sponsorship, reports that it has worked a drastic alteration on the mood of young people at such colleges as Smith, New Rochelle, Sarah Lawrence, and Williams. Having spoken in connection with the film myself, I can likewise testify to its potency in getting across to college students the truth about Communism. Moreover, the controversy over "Operation Abolition" has served to bring the whole Liberal-conservative struggle into the public eye. A typical experience is reported by Joseph McNally of Seton Hall University's Conservative Club, a YAF affiliate. "During February," he says, "we had a few requests for showings of the film and this gave us our initial publicity. March, April, and May were hectic, with the club showing the film three and four times a week. The question-and-answer periods after the film forced us to become 'experts' on the film, the House Committee, and conservative philosophy. The publicity we received caused us to be contacted by students from other local colleges who wanted to form conservative clubs of their own." And, in a significant afternote, McNally says:

These students were all younger than our group. This was the first ray of sunshine we had, because these young fellows were amazing. They were not the young faddists we expected. They were enthusiastic, intelligent, articulate young people who knew what they believed in and why. Two who stick out in my mind are Jay McNeill of St. Peter's College, Jersey City, and John Patten of Seton Hall. They are both 19-year-old sophomores who could take on anyone in the country in a debate on 'Operation Abolition' or HUAC and win hands down.

A Rutgers alumnus and a leader in YAF, Richard Plechner, reports similar results from a showing of the film at the New Brunswick school, as does young conservative Bob Malito at Queens.

In addition to its promotion of "Operation Abolition," YAF and its leaders have engaged in a variety of activities designed to strengthen the nation's internal security program. Two of its leaders, John and James Kolbe of Northwestern University, have formed a group called "The Student Committee for Congressional Autonomy." SCCA is aimed at vindicating the traditional right of Congress to engage in investigations, to inform itself and the public concerning the paramount issues before the nation. Focusing its first efforts on the battle over the Un-American Activities Committee, SCCA fired off letters to Congress in support of HUAC, arranged showings for "Operation Abolition," and distributed reports from the House Committee and the Senate Internal Security subcommittee. "The central issue," says John Kolbe, "has now become whether or not Congress will continue to investigate matters free of the arbitrary controls with which its opponents seek to shackle it. It is no longer an attack on one or two committees. They have declared war on both the congressional prerogative to inform itself and on the people's 'right to know.' "

YAF has also taken aggressive interest in the National Student Association, a Liberal-leaning group claiming to speak for American youth. One Young American for Freedom, Howard Phillips of Harvard, is head of the YAF-backed Student Committee for a Responsible National Student Organization. YAFers have tangled with NSA's Liberals on several occasions, the most notable of which was a 1961 rally staged in behalf of the Peace Corps. The young conservatives demanded that the proposed agency be made into a weapon against Communism, and have launched a national effort toward that end. Another conservative organization, the Committee for an Effective Peace Corps, has been laboring in this direction, under the leadership of Phillips and Tom Huston of Indiana University. (For further details on the conservative battle against NSA, See Chapter VIII.) YAF has taken a leaf from President Kennedy's book in maintaining a flurry of activity, launching new programs, issuing manifestoes, inundating the press with statements on public issues. It has very successfully "projected an image" of the new American right as it is, and promises increasingly to be: a center of dynamic energy, with the impulses spreading concentrically in all directions.

The group's most successful venture to date, and one which brought it considerable national attention, was a giant conservative rally staged in New York's Manhattan Center, in March of 1961. The purpose of the rally was to give awards, "for contributions to American conservatism and the youth of the nation," to eleven individuals and institutions. The recipients were James Abstine, Chairman of the Indiana College Young Republicans, Bill Buckley, Novelist Taylor Caldwell, Professor Russell Kirk, industrialist Herbert Kohler, publisher Eugene Pulliam, columnist George Sokolsky, Former AEC

Chairman Lewis Strauss, the House Un-American Activities Committee, the McGraw-Edison Company, and the Republic of China. Main speaker of the evening: Barry Goldwater.

To salute this constellation of conservatives, something over three thousand people assembled in Manhattan Center. Six thousand more, it was announced, had to be turned away. Outside, angry pickets protested the award to the House Un-American Activities Committee. The high point of the evening was the introduction of Goldwater. "Senator Goldwater's appearance," reported *The New York Times*, "set off a tumultuous ovation from the 3,200 persons crowded inside the center. . . . The crowd came to its feet as the Senator appeared. Hundreds of yellow, pink, and blue balloons stamped with his name filled the air, their colors picked out by roving spotlights. 'We Want Barry! We Want Barry!' the audience shouted, and the rhythm was picked up by a marching band in front of the stage. Huge placards with the Senator's picture waved over their heads. Knots of other spectators, most of them apparently students, thrust up signs telling of their schools or affiliation: 'Bay Ridge YAF,' 'Newton College,' 'Radcliffe,' 'The Bronx.' "

The meeting had a powerful impact, one way or another, on all who attended. As one mirthful conservative remarked, it was the sheer audacity of the enterprise which made it so enjoyable. It was, indeed, an audacious undertaking, so much so that it excited wide coverage in the New York papers, on the wire services, and in *Time* magazine. But all who were impressed were not happy with what they saw.

Criticism soon flowed from such Liberal journals as *The Commonweal* and *The Progressive*—and from such Communist-lining journals as *The National Guardian*. "War was the rally theme," exclaimed Mike Newberry in the Communist *Worker*. "Chiang Kai-shek's envoy, G.K.C. Yeh, set the mood by declaring that 'peaceful coexistence is an old Communist trick,' and the 'only hope for survival lies in victory,' not peace. The Young Americans for Freedom gave Mr. Yeh a 'Freedom Award' for 'International Affairs' in honor of his warmongering."

Murray Kempton of the *New York Post,* usually capable of a lighthearted *bonhommie* when inspecting conservative phenomena, also lapsed into surly invective. "The Young Americans for Freedom are only five months old," he noted, "yet they were able to put four thousand children into Manhattan Center Friday for an 'Homage to Barry Goldwater Night.' I cannot remember any agitational expression doing quite so well—which means quite so uncomfortably—at Manhattan Center since the Fur Workers in the late forties, so, by this standard, we must assume that the conservative revival is *the* youth movement of the sixties, and may even be as important to its epoch as the Young Communist League was to the thirties, which was not very."

Kempton rebuked YAF Director Caddy for referring to Mrs. Franklin D. Roosevelt as "Eleanor." "It was at first somewhat disturbing to sit in the presence of a young man who could refer to a great-grandmother he does not know by her first name, but one makes adjustments. I am ready to certify that young Master Caddy's manners are not worse than Jack Kerouac's."

The *Post's* columnist could not seem to find enough words to express his distaste. "For a middle-aged man," he added, "it could not be a total loss; in a child-oriented society, it is delightful to be free to hate children." He next referred to his hosts as "brats," berated their "arrogance," denounced them as humorless, declared their "posture . . . infuriating, their rhetoric deplorable." His vocabulary hostage to his loathing,

Kempton began striking off sentences of uncertain meaning: "Their prosody is of the sort which both reminds me and consoles me that my taste is better than my prose style." ("Prosody" would suggest the Young Americans for Freedom delivered their speeches in verse, which I am reliably informed they did not.) "Morgan Moulder, Chairman apparent of the House Un-American Activities Committee, was immediately recognizable as a patriot who arrived upon the podium after dining quite wisely but all too well." (This from an arbiter of political manners.) "I cannot quote William F. Buckley; he is ineluctable in type." ("Ineffable" may be the word for which Kempton was reaching.)

All in all, a sad performance from a usually entertaining and sometimes tolerant columnist. One speculates upon the reasons for so inflexible a display of "hatred," and for the collapse into spasms of incoherence. Psychoanalyzing the opposition, of course, is a game at which any number can play, but I shall be venturesome enough to suggest a reason for Mr. Kempton's inarticulate effort: his response is precisely that of the *ancien régime* to a new and incomprehensible force. Every orthodoxy tends to carve up the universe into certain defined categories, in which everything has a given place, and is expected to stay there. In the categories of Liberalism, youth belongs on the left. Conservatism is the purview of feeble codgers resistant to change. This is the typical view of Liberalism, and has been the explicit view of Kempton himself (who once described the conservative movement as notable for its advanced "state of wither").

When categories no longer hold, the universe loses its certainty. Uncertainty breeds fear, and fear breeds incoherence. Mr. Kempton's hatred for the "children" at Manhattan Center, I suggest, is the reflex of a mind which cannot grasp the altered structure of reality.

VII

The Young Republicans

> "I am quite prepared to write off the well-
> bred, frightened, bridge-playing women of Boise,
> Idaho, but I am not willing to surrender to
> either Nixon or Goldwater the potential young
> leaders at schools like the University of Indiana."
>
> JAMES A. MICHENER

THAT SO MANY officers of Young Americans for
Freedom are also leaders in the Young Republican movement is
neither conspiracy nor accident. Over the past decade, and particularly over the last five years, the YRs have become a strongly
conservative organization. In fact, stirrings of conservative
sentiment appeared in the Young GOP well before they were
evident elsewhere. When it came time for the launching of
YAF, several of these conservative young Republicans threw
in with the program, seeing it as a parallel venture to their
work in the YRs.

The Young Republican organization has not always displayed so independent, or so conservative, a spirit. During its
early years, it tended simply to reflect dominant Republican
policy—partially because it was not fully recognized as an autonomous element within the party, partially because ideology
seemed less important in those days. But as the YRs grew into

an active, cohesive force, and as young people became more sensitive to issues, things began to change. Today, the YRs are an autonomous, and conservative, force in Republican and national politics.

YR predispositions, and the senior party's sensitivity to them, are suggested by New York Governor Nelson Rockefeller's failure to show up at the last Young GOP convention. As *Time* magazine put it, "Rockefeller prudently refused an invitation to share the stage with Nixon and Goldwater at a National Young Republican conference this summer—a rally where every hemidemisemiquaver of applause will be carefully measured." And, at Young Republican national gatherings, the hemidemisemiquavers for Rockefeller are few and far between.

This now potent movement, with more than half-a-million members, has a continuous active history of only fifteen years or so, most of it conservative. The official beginnings date to June of 1931, when a National Conference of Young Republicans assembled in Washington's Willard Hotel. Approximately three hundred young people from all parts of the country, including the late Senator Robert A. Taft, were in attendance. This meeting was succeeded by the National Young Republican Organizations for Hoover, which created YR cadres in forty-five states, and led to the formation of a Young Republican National Committee. That group, late in 1935, launched what is now known as the Young Republican National Federation. J. Kenneth Bradley of Connecticut was elected permanent chairman—first of many important GOP names to emerge from YR politics.

The YRNF held its first convention in June, 1936. The meeting was addressed by a Young Republican named Styles Bridges, who also happened to be Governor of New Hampshire, and who went on to become a United States Senator.

Bradley was elected to the chairmanship over a YR from Minnesota, Harold Stassen, who had been nominated by Walter J. Mahoney, now majority leader of the New York State Senate. Stassen himself had nominated Gordon Allott of Colorado, currently the senior United States Senator from that state. On that occasion Allott withdrew; later, in 1941, he was elected to the chairmanship.

The federation had hardly gotten into motion when World War II intervened and brought domestic politics to a virtual standstill. It was in 1946, at the first post-war convention in Charleston, W. Va., that the YRNF began its career as a force in American politics, and that the story of its present conservatism really begins. It was in that year that the Republican National Committee officially recognized the group as the agency through which it would work with young people, and allocated office space to it in Republican headquarters. Ralph Becker of New York was elected chairman at a special convention in May, 1946, and re-elected to a full two-year term the following year. He was succeeded, in June 1949, by John Tope of Michigan. Both were to figure in the skirmishing which grew into a full-fledged ideological battle within the organization.

The Dewey defeat of 1948, and the Taft-Eisenhower battle of 1952, introduced a Liberal-Conservative rift in YR ranks which has yet to be fully resolved. As the 1951 YR convention approached, the group was split between adherents of Taft and Dewey. In preparation for the Republican convention of 1952, the Deweyites had begun moving toward General Eisenhower. The YR gathering was a test of strength between the two factions—and, as it developed, provided an accurate forecast of the senior convention which followed.

John Tope, who sided discreetly with the Dewey-Eisenhow-

er wing, presided over a convention in Boston's Hotel Statler
in June 1951 which was watched carefully by the press and by
senior Republicans as an indicator of party sentiment. The
principal candidates were Merrill Davis of Utah, representing
the Taft faction, and Herbert Warburton, chairman of the
Delaware Young Republicans, representing the Eisenhower
faction. (Davis was then a leader in the Utah legislature;
Warburton was later to become congressman from Delaware.)

The battle had little ideological clarity, if any, but the organizational lines were drawn clearly enough. Davis was backed
by Ralph Becker, who was close to the late Congressman, and
former GOP national chairman, Carroll Reece. Reece, a loyal
Taft follower, brought pressures to bear in behalf of Davis.
On the other side, Hugh Scott, then a congressman and now
senator from Pennsylvania, was among those working to line
up sentiment for Warburton.

Also behind Warburton was an influential group of Young
Republican leaders from Thomas E. Dewey's New York—F.
Clifton White, William A. Rusher and Charles K. McWhorter.

With the lines thus drawn, the convention wrangled through
five ballots to elect Warburton chairman, 246 to 215. The
Dewey-Eisenhower wing was in control, and the YRs assumed
a mildly "modernist" coloration. The same faction remained
dominant through the 1953 and 1955 conventions, when Sul-
livan Barnes of South Dakota and Charles McWhorter of New
York, respectively, succeeded to the chairmanship.

It should be stressed that, in the course of these factional
fights, a number of conservative YRs wound up on the Dewey-
Eisenhower side of things. Many were caught up in the belief
that "Taft couldn't win," and shared the mood of those of
their elders determined to end a twenty year Republican

drought. They believed that Eisenhower in office would perform as a conservative.

When the new administration got into motion, these young conservatives soon realized how mistaken they had been. The regime of Eisenhower, Sherman Adams and Herbert Brownell assiduously steered the party and the country leftward. The national administration moved increasingly toward "modernism," catered to Arthur Larson and Harold Stassen, and produced proposals for federal aid and foreign aid. Government spending increased and national resistance to Communism faltered. A number of conservative YRs took alarm. Their pragmatic option for Eisenhower had led to grief.

As this realization dawned, a conservative uprising began to take shape. A preliminary turning point came in the 1955 convention in Detroit, when McWhorter was elected chairman. The choice for co-chairman fell, with New York's approval, to Joyce Bovik of Colorado, whose Taft connections were in good order, and who was in favor with Carroll Reece. The choice opened the way for a rapprochement between the old Taft elements and a number of the conservative Young Republicans who had belonged to the Dewey apparatus. Joyce Bovik's election signalled the first move toward conservatism by the dominant group inside the YRNF and an entente between Reece and various YR leaders in New York.

The 1957 convention saw the first strong thrust of this new coalition—with results that sent shock tremors all the way to 1600 Pennsylvania Avenue. Principal contestants for chairman were John Ashbrook of Ohio and John Rousselot of California—who are now both in Congress, and who stand together on most roll calls as outspoken conservatives. Rousselot withdrew before the balloting, and the real battle of the convention came

to revolve around the selection of a co-chairman. The opposing candidates were Roseann Biwer of Wisconsin and Jerrie
Kent of Tennessee, the latter administrative assistant to Congressman Reece. As it happened, both were conservatives; but
Jerrie Kent's decision to run put squarely to the YR leaders
the problem of how much they were willing to cooperate with
the Taft-Reece wing of the party. The majority chose to go
with Kent, who won an easy victory on the first ballot. The
YR "team" was now clearly on the conservative track.

The 1959 convention featured an abortive attempt by friends
of New York's Liberal GOP Governor, Nelson Rockefeller,
to make some headway in the organization. The Rockefeller
effort never got off the ground, and an avowed Nixon backer
and conservative, Ned Cushing of Kansas, was elected chairman. As between Nixon and Rockefeller, there was little question as to where the YRs' sentiments lay. That preference was
made explicit by the fact that New York's delegation, normally
the keystone of a winning candidate's strength, was on the
outside looking in when the ballots were finally counted.
Cushing was carried into power by a solid coalition of Southern, Midwestern, and Far West states, winning, rather pointedly, without the votes of New York and a number of Liberal
delegations which had thrown in with the Empire State.

The new mood of the Young Republicans is revealed in
the increasingly conservative platforms they have adopted.
Through the 1955 convention, these documents tended to
reflect whatever policies happened to prevail at the senior level.
The 1955 platform, for example, contained the phrase, "we
commend the Eisenhower administration," or something of
the sort, no less than twenty-one times. Planks therein included
one saying, "We favor the stand of the Eisenhower administration to furnish aid in school construction to those districts

unable to properly provide their own construction because of lack of local revenues." It endorsed programs of medical care for the aged, and enacted a labor plank notable for its softness toward the demands of union leaders, and for its conspicuous silence on the glaring abuses even then obvious in such unions as the Teamsters and the UAW. The platform, in short, was a docile echo of the me-tooism of the senior party. If "modern" Republicanism was a carbon of the New Deal, the YRs were a second carbon.

The 1957 convention changed all this. Giving the nation its first look at the growing conservatism of the young, the YRs struck out on their own. An open revolt developed against the pallid "we commends" which had marked previous platforms. In a series of floor fights, the young GOP adopted militantly conservative planks on education, labor, foreign aid, cultural exchanges, and Communist China.

On federal aid to education, the stand of 1955 was reversed. "Mindful of the inevitable connection between subsidization and control," the convention declared, "we are unalterably opposed to federal financial aid for general public education and school construction."

On foreign aid: "We oppose all military assistance to Communist nations."

On cultural exchanges: "We recognize the dangers implicit in an indiscriminate expansion of so-called cultural exchanges with Communist governments whose true purpose is the degradation of all culture and the extinction of freedom itself."

On status-of-forces treaties: "We . . . recommend that our government re-examine the various status-of-forces agreements with the purpose of insuring that the American flag and all it stands for will protect each member of our armed forces, even as they are defending this nation and the Constitution."

On right to work laws: "We urge that the Taft-Hartley law be amended to prohibit compulsory union membership as a condition of employment."

On all four issues, the YRs took a stand diametrically opposed to that the of Eisenhower administration. The effect was sensational; the platform, normally a matter of insipid routine, wound up on the front pages of the *New York Times:* "Young GOP Hits Eisenhower Stand on Four Out of Five Issues." The floor fight had been hectic, but the conservative position had carried with votes to spare. The YRs were well on the road to conservatism.

They continued their travels two years later, at the 11th biennial convention in Denver. That gathering reaffirmed the YR's determination to think for themselves. In a show of intransigent self-reliance, the young GOP:

1. Came out overwhelmingly in opposition to federal aid to education, ignoring protests that the action was a "slap in the face" to the Eisenhower administration.

2. Shouted through an angry motion of censure against Senators Margaret Chase Smith of Maine and William Langer of North Dakota—both Republicans—for their votes against conservative Lewis Strauss as Secretary of Commerce.

3. Loudly booed Chief Justice Earl Warren when one delegate referred to him as a "great American," then declared that the effects of Supreme Court decisions "may legitimately be open to criticism and legislative alteration."

Among the platform planks and resolutions was the following on "summit" conferences:

"Resolved, that this convention goes on record in opposition to American participation in a 'summit' conference with the leaders of the Soviet Union, until such time as there is tangible evidence that the Communist regime is ready to honor its diplomatic agreements as a civilized nation."

One "modernist" delegate arose in consternation. "But the wording of this," he protested, "means there would *never* be a 'summit' conference with the Soviet Union!" The resolution's backers, as the saying goes, owned the soft impeachment. The motion was shouted through to approval.

Other planks and resolutions included:

On social security: "We believe that basic protection against loss of income should be provided by private means and that the old age and survivor's program should be a supplementary source of help to those who cannot otherwise help themselves."

On public power: "Present public power projects should not be expanded but restricted to their present scope. We believe that public power projects should be gradually returned to private enterprise wherever feasible."

On labor: "We affirm our support of section 14 (b) of the Taft-Hartley law ... and urge making labor unions subject to anti-trust statutes ... outlawing all forms of so-called organizational blackmail picketing ... strengthening present prohibitions against secondary boycotts."

Other resolutions adopted at Denver included demands for "elimination of governmental subsidies to inefficiencies in agriculture"; a budget surplus, aimed at retiring the national debt; a reform of the graduated income tax; strict enforcement of laws pertaining to political activities by labor unions; and endorsement of H.R. 3, a bill to restore state sedition laws struck down by the Supreme Court in 1956.

Summing up the convention, Chairman Cushing said: "There is a steady trend to conservatism in America today, and we think the Young Republicans are helping to show the way. The platform we adopted in Denver this summer was the most conservative in the history of the federation. It shows that the YRs take their stand for principle, not expediency."

The YRs have also adopted a number of resolutions on particular occasions, as when at their executive committee meeting in Reno, in May, 1960, they issued a strongly-worded condemnation of the Communist-led riots against the House Un-American Activities Committee, and urged the continuation of U-2 flights over the Soviet Union.*

Conservative Victory: A Case History

At the college level, the young Republicans have similarly led the way in the resurgence of conservative activity. The College Service Committee of the federation is strongly influenced by the politics of its largest and most active constituent member—the Midwest Federation of College Young Republican Clubs. In consequence, this group has become a contested battleground for conservative and Liberal factions. In 1960, with an unprecedented five hundred delegates in attendance at Des Moines, Iowa, the Liberal faction had triumphed; but, in 1961, with more than one thousand delegates on hand in St. Paul, Minnesota, the conservatives swept back into power. The conservative victory was all the more impressive because it was achieved against monumental odds.

The convention was held on the home grounds of the outgoing Liberal chairman. The Liberals' main strength was to

---

* In the matter of platforms and policy resolutions, the YRs continued their rightward journey at their 1961 national convention in Minneapolis. The delegates once more declared their opposition to federal aid to education, urged resumption of America's nuclear test program, recommended a total trade embargo against the Communist empire, and asked that America withdraw financial support from the United Nations—and consider withdrawing membership—if Red China were admitted to it. All three candidates for national chairman advertised themselves as "conservatives," and the resulting fissure allowed the least conservative of the three to gain election. At the college level, the results were clearer, as Northwestern University student James Harff was elected chairman. "The conscience of a conservative," Harff said in an obvious reference to Senator Barry Goldwater's book, "has certainly spoken at this convention."

come from Minnesota, Michigan and the Dakotas—all geographically convenient to St. Paul. Conservative strength centered in Indiana, Illinois, Iowa, and Kansas.

The convention boiled down to a question in logistics: how
to get enough conservative delegations on the scene to counter-
act the powerful advantage the Liberals gained by having control of the convention machinery, and of holding the meeting
on their home grounds. The magnitude of the problem is suggested by the fact that better than 240 delegates were certified
as eligible from Minnesota alone.

The conservatives went about the task of raising enough
money to take their delegations to St. Paul by bus. Two buses
each travelled from Indiana and Illinois, supplying upwards of
a hundred delegates apiece. One bus came from Kansas. Automobile caravans brought delegates from Iowa, Missouri, and
Nebraska.

When the convention got into motion, Friday, April 14, no
less than one thousand delegates were on hand—to contest control of just one section of a college political organization!

The conservative candidate was James H. Abstine of Indiana, a Republican in the Goldwater mold, and a recipient
of a Young Americans for Freedom award at the YAF rally in
March. His opponent was Pete McPherson of Michigan, who
had distinguished himself ideologically by coming out for repeal of the Connally Reservation.

Having surmounted their disadvantages in geography, the
Abstine forces drew their battle plan sharply along ideological
lines. Abstine had begun his attack in December, 1960, following an executive committee meeting in which conservative
efforts had been rebuked by the regime in power. "Matters of
the utmost importance to Young Republicans in the colleges
and universities in the Midwest and through the nation," he

said, "were brought to light as a result of the recent meeting of the Midwest board. There is a general agreement among observers of that meeting that left-wing and extremist Liberal elements within the Midwest and possibly in several other areas are maneuvering to seize control of the Midwest Federation of College Young Republican clubs in 1961, and if successful there, to grab the College Service Committee of the YRNF."

The goal of "the most extreme members of this clique," he charged, was to build Nelson Rockefeller "for the presidential nomination of the Republican Party in 1964 to the preclusion of consideration of Vice-President Nixon, Senator Goldwater, or any person within this party."

Abstine cited a number of record votes on matters of ideology: a proposal to endorse the Sharon Statement of YAF; appointment of Philip Jessup, of the left-wing Institute of Pacific Relations, to the World Court; and the Connally Reservation. On these issues, he pointed out, the dominant bloc, which included his opponent-to-be, McPherson, voted the Liberal position—against the Sharon Statement, for Jessup, against the Connally Reservation.

Abstine's adherents formed a nucleus of conservative strength at St. Paul. They were joined by conservatives from all over the Midwest, who understood the significance of the convention—as did the senior GOP. In effect, the battle was a test of strength between the followers of Nelson Rockefeller and of Barry Goldwater. As the convention got under way, Abstine's partisans began a literature bombardment to draw attention to his unyielding conservatism, citing his stand on Red China, the House Un-American Activities Committee, federal aid to education. The Liberals ducked for cover, and tried to convince wavering delegates that they, too, were "conservatives."

A head count of the convention early Saturday morning revealed the balance of power was tipping to the conservatives—how much so as yet unclear. The Abstine forces found themselves confronted with yet another obstacle. The credentials committee, controlled by the Liberal opposition, industriously set about to disqualify as many delegations as possible known to be leaning to Abstine. The final balloting was delayed for hours by these strenuous exertions. By the time the credentials committee was ready to report, better than sixty-five conservative delegates found themselves disqualified.

The showdown came on a vote as to whether the disinherited delegates were to be seated. On a division of the house, the Abstine forces, who had staked their entire campaign on conservatism, carried the motion by a margin of better than seventy votes. The Liberals, acknowledging that they were beaten, withdrew altogether. Abstine was elected by acclamation.

The Wisconsin *Daily Cardinal,* not always noted for its friendship to the conservative cause, gave a summary of the convention so plainspoken as to be worth quotation at length. In an editorial headed, "The Key to The GOP—Conservatism on the Rise," the *Cardinal* said:

Had our newest columnist R. E. Fauber been shanghaied and dragged raging off to the Midwestern Regional conference of the National Young Republicans in St. Paul this past weekend, he would've picked up another magic incantation to add to his list printed in Saturday's *Daily Cardinal.* The password and key to success with the Midwestern Young Republicans was "conservative." Their adherence to this word was surprisingly strong and complete.

All an applause-hungry speaker had to do in order to receive a thundering ovation was to bellow something like, "We're all conservatives here!" and down would come the rafters. Dropping Senator Barry Goldwater's name produced an even bigger roar.

Of the two candidates running for regional chairman, one, the eventual winner, was an avowed conservative; the other was originally pegged as a Liberal or Rockefeller Republican, but by the time for voting he had managed to squirm further and further to the right until he was sitting on Senator Goldwater's lap.

Governor Andersen of Minnesota was booed and hissed when he discussed his programs in terms of Liberal Republicanism. Things even got so thick that when one speaker dared mention the name of Rockefeller, the only response was a loud, resounding belch from the floor, plus a few embarrassed titters.

Wisconsin's part in this conservative upswing was influential, mainly through the organ of *Insight and Outlook*. Most of the delegates had heard about the magazine, and many even read it regularly. When reprints of articles and extra copies were passed out the supplies were soon exhausted. *Insight's* executive editor (and *Cardinal* columnist) Richard S. Wheeler was nearly as well known as many of the delegation leaders.

All this points down one road: these delegates from Wisconsin, Minnesota, North and South Dakota, Kansas, Nebraska, Oklahoma, Missouri, Iowa, Illinois, Indiana, Michigan, and Ohio were sold solid on the tenets of Conservatism as preached by Senator Goldwater. Since it is these people who will be representing the "grass roots" in the 1962 and '64 campaigns, we can expect a strong swing to the right from Midwest Republicans in these coming years.

This influence does not stop here, either. We heard a group of Republican state senators from Minnesota commenting favorably on the popularity and strength of the conservative movement which the Midwest Young Republicans had shown that day. Other leaders were similarly impressed with the strength of the movement.

If this conservative enthusiasm continues to mount, and there's no reason to [believe] that it will not, we can expect to see it completely sweep the Midwest Republican party. Unless the Liberal Republicans do some fast moving, conservatism is the bandwagon to join in the Midwest.

The episode indeed established that conservatism was the "bandwagon to join." It further established that, even at the college level, young conservatives are not simply ideologues spouting slogans; they understand the realities of practical politics, and are willing to work hard to put their views into effect. And it proved the value of the extensive personal contacts established by travelling evangelists of conservatism, who had contacted the various conservative leaders on the individual campuses, and had helped sew them together into a cohesive movement.

Further evidences of YR conservatism may be found by reviewing the progress of individual states. The chairman of the Massachusetts YRs, Michael Robbins, is an outspoken conservative. "The hope of the Republican Party," he says, "and of the nation, is in a steadfast loyalty to the principles of limited government and national sovereignty. The shibboleths of Liberalism have been proved false by the test of events. Young people are turning increasingly to the conservative standard, both on the campus and beyond it."

Similar pronouncements could be quoted from innumerable other YR chairmen across the nation—most notably in the Midwest and the South. The increasing influence of the GOP in Dixie, in fact, may be attributed in large part to the conjunction of those two elements—conservative principle, and the growing appetite of young people for politics. During the 1960 campaign, the Young Republican Chairman of North Carolina observed that "the younger generation is more attracted to the conservative cause than that generation which attained adulthood during the hey-day of the New Deal."

The North Carolinians have also read a lecture to their elders on the subject of me-tooism. In their official platform for 1961, they state:

"History shows plainly that when the fundamental beliefs of a political party become vague and nebulous, then it loses its hold upon the imagination and loyalty of the people and soon ceases to exist. We see no future for the Republican Party in a position of easy opportunism professing to be all things to all men."

Elsewhere in the South, similar comment has come from the YRs of Texas—a state which, like North Carolina, has experienced a strong surge of Republican sentiment in recent years. *The Contact,* the Texas YR newsletter, says: "To succeed in Texas we must entice conservative Democrats into our ranks, and direct our approach toward the younger generation. Generally opposed to centralized federal government increases, heavy taxes and deficit spending, this young generation is just now assuming the roles of leadership."

Proving their fealty to their principles, the Texas YGOP came up with a platform plank urging the state legislature to turn down federal grants-in-aid. "We know this will be inconvenient," they said, "because we will still be required to pay Washington our share of these federal programs. But we call to the attention of the people of Texas that the problem is not one of financing, but one of the continued power and factual independence of the state of Texas."

The story of Texas' YRs is instructive in other ways—suggesting that the conservative effort within the YRs has not been aimed simply at make-believe victories in a facsimile of politics. The conservatives have been, by and large, conscious that their objective is to influence, not simply the YR organization, but the course of American government as a whole. In consequence, they have worked hard in behalf of conservative candidates for office.

A determined young man named John Berke has, at twenty-six, left his mark on the politics of Texas. Assuming leadership of the State Young GOP in late 1960, he launched or galvanized no less than thirty-five YR clubs in the space of a few months—bringing the total of active groups from six to forty-one. An outspoken conservative, Berke vanquished a lingering contingent of Liberals, and took his state's delegation to the 1961 National YR convention to work for a conservative victory. In the course of all this, he mobilized the YR organization into a massive effort in behalf of Senator John Tower, the Goldwater-style Republican who made political history in 1961. He has also turned his energetic workers out in behalf of the GOP's lone Texas congressman, conservative Bruce Alger, who represents Berke's native Dallas.

Equally important, the YRs themselves have been graduating into the ranks of senior party politics. And, as suggested by the examples of Bridges, Taft, Allott, and Mahoney, it often develops that Young Republicans become men of consequence in party counsels. In the 87th Congress, no less than thirty-two GOP Congressmen were under the age of forty—nineteen of them freshmen, almost all of them conservatives. An outstanding example is John Ashbrook of Ohio, former chairman of the YRNF, who at thirty-two became the youngest Republican in Congress. Ashbrook campaigned on an uncompromisingly conservative platform, and was elected by a heavy majority. He made extensive use of voting records compiled by organizations which monitor Congress—ranging in sympathy from conservative to ultra-Liberal—to prove his opponent had voted consistently in favor of increased spending, higher taxes, and inflation.

A typical Ashbrook stand was expressed in a letter he fired off to William Schnitzler, Secretary-Treasurer of the AFL-CIO, concerning the Forand bill for medical care to the aged. Schnitzler had threatened to crucify candidates who would not come out for the bill. Ashbrook's rejoinder: "I for one am opposed to Forand-type health insurance and the attempt to tie it to the social security system. . . . It is compulsory, a type of social-ized medicine; it is not equated to need. . . ." Moreover, he said, "the continued efforts of yourself and many other leaders to drive a wedge between the worker and the rest of the citi-zenry is disturbing. . . . The worker is vitally interested in the integrity of the dollar and combatting inflation. He wants his pension fund worth something when the time comes for retire-ment. . . . The worker is also vitally interested in preserving what is left of the free enterprise system and he categorically rejects socialism. He knows that the cost of your gigantic wel-fare programs may ultimately destroy both the integrity of the dollar and the free enterprise system."

This intransigence caused one newspaper in Ashbrook's dis-trict to offer the hopeful but melancholy observation that "he is a man of conservative principle in a period when conservatism is seeking and in rare instances finding, new and badly-needed leaders. It is a period, too, when conservatism is basically a defensive position, a position of resistance against the powerful and, we fear, disastrous march of welfarism and socialism."

Ashbrook's victory, however, suggests that conservatism may not be so defensive as the editorialist feared—that the rebellion of youth against its Liberal professoriate is already being felt in the halls of Congress. That optimistic conclusion is sup-ported by another freshman congressman, John Rousselot of California, a former YR associate of Ashbrook's and, next to Ashbrook, the youngest Republican in the House. Rousselot credits his present conservatism to his Liberal professors. "Be-cause of their propaganda," he says, "I began to think about the questions of governing power. . . . Most of them believed in socialism. After years in business and in government, I see how wrong they were. The longer I live, the more I realize that socialism, instead of alleviating the sufferings of humanity, as we are led to believe, will only lead to destruction of our nation. A limited government is a freer government, and coupled with free enterprise, is the only way we can have any real progress."

The voters of Rousselot's district (once represented by Richard Nixon) apparently agreed with this view—since they put Rousselot into office by a margin of some twenty-four thousand votes. And his fellow GOP freshmen also seem to concur, having elected him chairman of the "87th Club," the caucus of first-term Republican congressmen.

A third young Republican congressman in the new mold is Donald Bruce of Indiana, who won election to the House from the city of Indianapolis at the age of thirty-nine. Representing an industrial city of some half-million people, Bruce owns one of the most impeccably conservative voting records in Congress, and proudly uses the word "conservative" in his campaign literature. He staked his election chances on proving that his opponent was a Liberal—and, like Ashbrook, established the point with voting records from COPE, ADA, Americans for Constitutional Action, and Civic Affairs Associates.

"I think we have to vote our principles here," says Don Bruce. "Someone has to take a stand for conviction somewhere along the line, or the country is going to be soon bankrupt, and our freedoms will go glimmering." Will his conservative voting record hurt him at the polls? "I don't think so," Bruce answers. "I believe there is a conservative resurgence in our district, as there is in the country generally. My mail ran heavily against the effort to pack the House Rules Committee, by a margin of better than ten-to-one. I have been particularly encouraged by the response of the young people; in speaking to them in groups, talking with them during my trips home and here at the office, I have been greatly impressed with their grasp of the issues. They understand that freedom is at stake and they are increasingly rallying to the conservative cause."

VIII

The Battle Against NSA

"The essence of all Babbittry, senior or junior,
is stereotypes. The stereotypes of Babbitt Senior
are the following words and connotations: solid,
reliable, sound, businesslike, wholesome, and
knows-how-to-meet-a-payroll. Junior's stereotyped
words and connotations are: vital, dynamic, func-
tional, unpuritanical, forward-looking, the masses,
and the common man."

PETER VIERECK

NO SURVEY OF CAMPUS POLITICS can be complete, or
even relatively accurate, without some discussion of a group
known as the United States National Student Association.
NSA, as it is more familiarly known, is frequently considered
to be the "voice" of American students. As such its political
complexion and its credentials of representation have considerable bearing on the present discussion.

NSA, founded in 1947 at the University of Wisconsin, is
an agglomeration of student government organizations. It
claims affiliations with anywhere from three hundred to four
hundred campuses, and a "membership" of 1.3 million students. Its principal concern—according to its constitution and
various utterances from its officials—is with the internal prob-

lems of the academic community. Its constitution stipulates that NSA is not supposed to range into matters of politics. Section A, Article 10 of that document states: "No body acting on behalf of USNSA shall participate in sectarian religious activities or partisan political activities; they shall not take part in activity which does not affect students in their role as students." Section B of the same article says: "No substantial part of the activities of the national and regional bodies of USNSA shall be devoted to carrying on propaganda or otherwise attempting to influence legislation."

Nevertheless, NSA spends a large part of its time participating in just those prohibited activities. The group has increasingly insinuated itself into political controversies—covering everything from nuclear testing to "colonialism in Mozambique"—striking off jargonistic policy statements in the name of "American students." NSA leaders apparently look upon the college years as an apprenticeship in politics and group manipulation, rather than a time for training the intellect (a fact which shows up rather prominently in NSA's literary efforts).*

This course is dictated, in the NSA view, by the canons

---

* It is perhaps unfair to demand perfect literacy of any publication, or of any writer. But NSA's record in this respect is so unusually bad that it warrants further comment. NSA pamphlets are clogged with awkward, indistinct terms—"community-structured unit" is an example—which betray indistinct ideas. A good deal of this jargon is borrowed from the graceless vocabulary of the socal scientists. Parts of some NSA publications are well-written, but the usual style is elephantine obscurity. For example, one passage from the *National Student News* reads: "Uncritical acceptance of majority positions or goals totally divorced from any feeling of personal commitment for their support or achievement and semi-fatalistic writing-off of such commitment as useless characterizes many if not most campuses and students."

As for grammar, there are few infinitives so tightly constructed that NSA cannot split them. A 1956 NSA working paper argues the need for a special subcommission *"to,* under the supervision of the National Office, *revise and bring up to date"* an NSA brochure called, of all of "interrelatedness"—meaning the relevance of everything to everything else, and thus the relevance to students of national and international affairs. Since classroom instruction does not always contribute to "intelligent citizenship," as one NSA president conceived it, "it seems all the more urgent that student government devote prime efforts toward the creation of an atmosphere conducive to developing student awareness and understanding of national and world situations."

If this policy meant simply a campaign to encourage "awareness" in general, criticism of NSA might be somewhat less vehement. But as a conduit for political ideas, the group has made it abundantly clear that to be Aware, one must also be Liberal. This fact, and the further fact that NSA claims to speak for *all* American students, must be measured against the signs of a conservative revival on the campus. Is NSA in fact Liberal? And if so, how representative is it of student sentiment throughout the country?

The answer is that, historically, NSA has been very Lib-

---

things, "Course Evaluation." The January, 1958 issue of the *News* tells us "student government control, responsibility and programming" are sometimes "non-existant," which might be viewed as a typographical error, had not the previous month's *News* disclosed that low-cost housing near UCLA was also "non-existant." The January issue also states, in a discussion of *Who's Who in American Colleges:* "Rather significant *is* the criteria used by colleges in selecting candidates for *Who's Who.*" A working paper put together in 1957 similarly notes that ours is "a privileged society, with *a* hollow criteria of success." Misspellings are also common. An NSA pamphlet explaining the "student bill of rights" quotes that document as holding certain conditions "indispensible" for a suitable education; a form letter "endorces" the Youth March for Integrated Schools; and a 1958 issue of the *National Student News* offers a quotation from "John Stewart Mill." Such errors would not have particular significance, if it were not for the fact that NSA, in addition to its total immersion in politics, has also proposed to take a hand in the shaping of the college curriculum.

eral indeed—well to the left of, say, the majority of the Democratic Party in America. This fact has been a source of comfort
to Liberals at the senior level. It is standard doctrine among
these gentry to argue that collectivism is "inevitable," because
each generation advances further to the left than its predecessor. Thus "youth," in the Liberal universe, should always be
to the left of its elders. The radicalism of NSA has fitted com-
fortably into these categories. Aging Liberals can point with
assurance to NSA's various pronouncements, as representing
the opinions of the coming generations.

The role thus assigned to NSA is not an easy one. In an age
when Liberalism is an entrenched orthodoxy, when the overwhelming majority of the faculty, the mass media, and the
government are aggregated on the left, it takes some effort to
be still more radical. But NSA has tried hard. It has, for example, come out repeatedly in favor of federal aid to education, against the discharge of Communist teachers, against
loyalty oaths for students in the Naval ROTC. At its 1960 "national congress," it called for the emasculation of the House
Un-American Activities Committee, asked abolition of the loyalty oath and disclaimer affidavit in the National Defense
Education Act, urged a "general suspension of nuclear testing," and condemned the "deplorable persecution of students
in the universities of Spain," while displaying a quizzical amity
for the "university reform" being conducted by the Communist
regime of Fidel Castro.

Additionally, NSA produced a startling expression of support for the Japanese students, led by Communists, who rioted
against President Eisenhower in June 1960. The resolution
stated:

Fact. During May and June of 1960, student demonstrations
occurred in Japan protesting the Japanese-American Security

Treaty and the methods employed by the Kishi cabinet to obtain its ratification.

Declaration. 1. In accordance with its recognition of the right of students to non-violently protest actions which they consider unjust or undemocratic, the USNSA upholds the expression of this right by Japanese students.

2. USNSA deplores the unfortunate incidents occurring due to police brutality and student violence . . . .

Nowhere in this resolution did NSA refer to the fact that the riots were Communist-inspired, that they were viciously anti-American, that they forced the calling off of a state visit by the President of the United States, or that they were scored as a humiliating defeat for America and a stunning propaganda victory for the Kremlin. To NSA's junior potentates, nothing was involved but the "rights" of Japanese students.

If those facts leave any lingering doubts that NSA lists noticeably to port, its record on the question of "federal aid" may provide further illumination. The organization's efforts on behalf of federal intervention in education have been nothing short of heroic. Ray Farabee, NSA president for the 1957-58 school year, went before the Senate Labor and Public Welfare Committee to urge federal aid to college students. The *National Student News,* NSA's official publication (now defunct) pounded away at the subject with unremitting zeal.

In five issues of the *News* I have before me as I write, there are no less than thirty-three separate stories dealing with finances—five of them in a special supplement entitled "Rising Costs Squeeze College Students." Of these articles, thirteen in one way or another promote the idea of federal assistance to college students. That works out to an average of four finance stories per issue, or more than six per issue if we average in the special supplement; and to better than two pro-federal aid stories per issue.

Such attitudes would seem to mean that, far from there being a "conservative revival" on America's campuses, students
are farther left than ever. The evidence suggests, however, that
NSA does not in fact speak for "American students" as such,
and indeed speaks for only a negligible portion of its own
claimed membership; NSA, in a word, has led its Liberal elders
to envision a future which exists only in the minds of NSA's
own top echelons. Moreover, not only has NSA served to veil
the existence of conservative sentiment on the campus, its
claims to representation, and its techniques for enforcing them,
have ignited conservatives into angry resistance. It is not too
much to say that NSA, through a sort of reverse impact, has
done a great deal to spur the conservative rebellion.

It should be noted that NSA sometimes argues that it is not
left-wing at all. I have frequently encountered this statement
from outraged devotees of the group. But if a steady campaign
for federal aid, a crusade against loyalty oaths and HUAC, and
an expression of support for Communist-led foreigners who
revile the American President are not "left" in American politics, then words have indeed lost their meaning.

NSA's second and somewhat more serious line of defense
is to acknowledge that its various stands add up to "Liberal"
or "left-wing," but to claim this is an authentic expression of
student sentiment. Commenting on one of my own criticisms
of the group, an NSA booster writes: "No one who has come
in contact with NSA can deny it is Liberal-oriented and no
doubt some would agree with Evans. But there are few . . . who
would call the majority of university students conservative."

NSA itself says: "Accurately reflecting the feelings of students on member campuses, USNSA's structure provides a representative organ for American students, despite the pluralistic
heterogeneity of the nation's system of higher education."

This assertion is challenged by conservative opponents of the group. Howard Phillips, president of the Harvard Student Council, says: "There are probably not a million students who have ever heard of NSA, and the number of individuals who can correctly identify it at all is most likely in the thousands." "NSA officials," Phillips adds, "will occasionally admit that their organization is not as close to students as it pretends to be, but such admissions are generally accompanied by the qualification that students active in NSA reflect student opinion nationally and comprise the 'real vanguard' of the student movement in the United States."

The basic organizational unit of NSA is the "region"—consisting of either one very large state, or two fair-sized ones, or several small ones. The NSA organizational chart carves the country up into twenty such regions. Each is allowed to establish its own constitution and mode of operation, within the framework of the national NSA constitution. Each elects a chairman and a vice-chairman: all the chairmen are members of the executive committee; in regions representing more than forty thousand students, the vice-chairman is also a member. There are five national officers—a president and four vice-presidents, all of whom are also members (non-voting) of the executive committee. This group of thirty-five people forms the "power elite" of NSA, and effectively determines its stance on issues.

Theoretically, NSA policy is established by delegates in convention assembled. Student critics charge, however, that these annual meetings are so stacked in favor of Liberalism that there can be little question of what the final result will be. For one thing, the ideological context in which delegates are asked to deliberate tends to insure a Liberal result. "According to NSA thinking," says Phillips, "the American student, sharing

his persecution with young scholars in other countries, is re-
garded as a member of an 'international student movement.'
As such, NSA participants are urged to consider issues, not
on the basis of American interests, but in the light of their
usefulness to 'the cause.' As a result, every resolution adopted
by the unwitting delegates is colored in some way with this
theory."

NSA's claim to accurate representation is further compromised by its habit of speaking as if its entire "membership"
(consisting of the aggregate student bodies of all affiliated
schools), or even all American students, endorsed its programs.
Many schools have affiliated with NSA without a referendum;
many others, referendum or no, have affiliated on grounds, generally concerning technical services, having nothing to do
with ideology. Many of the 1.3 million are thus unaware that
NSA even exists; and many others oppose its radical position
on issues. Yet, with the entire student body of an affiliated
school lumped into the NSA "membership," these young people
are, like it or not, "represented" by NSA's various pronouncements.

To make matters worse, say the rapidly-growing band of
NSA's student critics, the group's method of running its annual
conventions offers small chance of authentic representation.
Frequently "delegates" to an NSA congress are not elected
by their campuses, and many students have no idea that their
schools are sending representatives to these annual conclaves.
In other cases, the delegates are chosen on grounds having
nothing to do with their political beliefs, but are asked to pass
upon some of the most complicated and hotly disputed problems facing the nation. During the conventions, these matters
are discussed in speeches and literature heavily weighted toward

the left. "Research personnel" of the same tendency are brought in to leaven the proceedings with expertise. Committees gestating resolutions and mandates are kept under tight Liberal dominion. The fruits of their labor, amounting to several score motions on every conceivable subject, are then thrust upon the delegates, who are called upon to pass them with virtually no opportunity to weigh the pros and cons of the issues. When it is all over, the results are handsomely printed, and mailed around the world as the opinion of American youth. No minority reports are issued, and no minutes are presented to indicate that an opposing point of view has ever been ventilated at any point along the way.

A typical complaint about these proceedings comes from Bill Dalgetty, a student who, as President of the student body at the State University of Iowa, attended NSA's 1960 congress. It was obvious, Dalgetty charged, "that all discussion and legislation was deliberately directed to one point of view. Background and working papers from which delegates formulated their ideas and opinions represented only one side of the story. Resource personnel in many of the subcommittees and committees once again presented only one side of the question. This can be supported by the example of the subcommittee discussing the Japanese student riots. Only Japanese students who had participated in the riots were heard. On numerous occasions, the chair spoke on one side of the issue without relinquishing his position as presiding officer." Before the subcommittee meetings, Dalgetty says, the national officers talked to certain of the delegates, inquiring whether they knew "what they were to do, where they were to go, what resolutions they were to originate, and what resolutions they were to defeat." During the meetings, "in many instances, individuals from

the back of the room would spring up and write a profession-
ally worded resolution in a matter of minutes. Obviously it
had been thought out and written beforehand. . . ."

Here is the way an NSA Evaluation Committee, representing seven schools in the Illinois-Wisconsin region, sums up
the case against NSA:

1. All opinions coming from NSA appear to be *the* unanimous opinion of American students, whereas often there is
great controversy and the voting is close. Minority reports are
not published and the vote tally is not recorded with the resolution.

2. While it claims to represent all United States students
(in its preamble it states . . . . "We, *the* students of the United
States of America" . . .) NSA's total membership is only one-
third of the U. S. student population.

3. Delegates to its congresses are usually not elected, and even
where they are, it rarely is on a political platform.

4. Too often the national and regional congresses are not
run democratically (i.e., biased committee chairmen, one-
sided research material, and one-sided debates).

5. A small part of NSA's resolutions are voted upon by the
congresses. Almost two-thirds of its codification were voted
upon by the 35-member National Executive Committee, rather
than the representatives of its claimed 1,300,000 membership.

6. Member schools usually join through student governments, not by students voting in a referendum.

7. Few students are aware of their membership in NSA or
of what NSA really is and what it is saying for them.

8. NSA forfeits its representativeness by taking stands on too
many and varied issues, where students are uninformed or
apathetic (i.e., statements in the codification of policy range

from "the student and the total community" to "colonialism in Angola and Mozambique").

9. There is inadequate communication and distribution of pertinent materials among member schools of both the national and regional assemblies. (This includes follow-up on resolutions, actions and mandates of the NEC and the various regional executive committees.)

10. Members of the NEC do not necessarily represent the opinions of schools in the nation or from their regions. They often do not keep in touch with the member schools, do not confer with them before voting for them. (I.e., the Ill.-Wis. region had no meeting between the summer congress and the winter NEC meeting. The chairman had not contacted most member schools about any of the issues voted upon at the winter meeting.)

11. Even after the NEC passes resolutions, member schools are often unaware of the stands taken (i.e., resolutions passed in early September, 1960, reached member schools in late December 1960, or not at all. Minutes are not sent to member schools, even upon request. There is no way a member school can know how its regional chairmen voted, since a record of the vote is not kept.)

This writer can personally testify to the truth of the eleventh assertion—that "even after the NEC passes resolutions, member schools are often unaware of the stands taken." Indeed, it is clear that even *delegates* to NSA's national conventions are sometimes unaware of what has been enacted in their name. On one occasion in the fall of 1960, I was invited by students at a Midwestern university to give my views on NSA. The school was an NSA affiliate, but its student senate was reconsidering the value of the connection. The preceding week, I had written a piece calling attention to NSA's pronouncement in behalf of the Japanese rioters. I was confronted by a young lady with fire in her eye. She waved a copy of my column in my face—the paragraph concerning the Japanese resolution underlined. "I was at this convention," she declared, "and no such resolution was passed!" When I told her it had been enacted by the National Executive Committee, she expressed disbelief. Fortunately, a representative of NSA was on hand. Under questioning, he acknowledged to this NSA delegate, that, thanks to the National Executive Committee, she and better than a million other students were on record as sympathizing with the Japanese rioters.

This sort of ignorance apparently extends to the people who actually *do* vote on the resolutions. "Even members of the NEC," reports Kay Wonderlic of Northwestern University, "were unclear as to what they passed concerning Japan. Of three contacted during the four months since the Congress, one denied it was passed, one said he didn't know if it had been, and the other said a resolution to that effect was passed, but he couldn't recall specifics of it. Even as the NEC was unsure of its decisions, and members uninformed, copies of resolutions were sent around the world."

The technique of shoving controversial resolutions through the NEC—resolutions of which delegates and even NEC members are unaware—is perhaps the clearest evidence that NSA policies represent little more than the views of a few professional leaders. Miss Wonderlic comments:

All continuing policies of USNSA are incorporated in a Codification of Policies, which serves as the official statement of association policy. It is brought up to date each year after the congress by the National Executive Committee, subject to the approval of the next Congress. Resolutions passed at congresses remain in the codification as continuing policy unless amended or repealed by a two-thirds vote.

The Constitution states, "Resolutions of the NEC shall hereafter be included in the codification only by vote of the next congress." Resolutions of the post-congress NEC meeting are actually included in the codification immediately after passage. Eighty-six such resolutions are in the 1960-61 codification. The 1960-61 president of NSA, Dick Rettig, explains this by saying these resolutions are referred to the National Executive Committee by committees of the congress and therefore should not be considered NEC resolutions. He did not comment on the fact that the NEC may alter and completely change the meaning of the resolutions, as well as vote final passage or failure.

Passage of resolutions by the NEC is NSA's favored technique for putting itself on record concerning controversial issues. At the 1960 NSA congress, ninety-five resolutions were worked up for consideration by five committees. Only thirteen of these were considered by the plenary session. The remaining eighty-two resolutions, plus seventeen other motions, were passed along to the NEC. Out of these ninety-nine items, eighty-two were passed. Final score for the proceedings: congress, ten; NEC, eighty-two. Four resolutions which had not been referred to the NEC by committee were passed and included in the codification. So was a "program mandate" (instructions to the NSA staff for carrying out policy).

A number of students have battled NSA on their individual campuses. At Indiana University, Tom Huston, president of the Conservative League and a member of the student senate, has waged a campaign to end the school's affiliation with NSA. Speaking in behalf of Indiana University's Inter-Fraternity Council, Huston accused the group of falsely using its membership statistics to "muster prestige" in behalf of Liberal policies. Huston's efforts led the university student senate to conduct a re-evaluation of NSA, with eye-opening results for many students who knew little of the organization. Indiana University subsequently called for reforms within the group and declared that otherwise the school might reconsider its membership.

At Stanford University, students Thomas Reilly and Richard Noble participated in a successful battle to keep NSA from being re-introduced on the campus. At Harvard, Howard Phillips has led an effective battle against the group. In Colorado, Stan Dempsey, a young conservative leader, has done a great deal to expose NSA's organizational inequities. At Dunbarton College, Carol Bauman led the fight; at Northwestern, Kay Wonderlic, Vice-President of the Student Senate, presented a telling indictment of the group's "undemocratic" techniques. At Butler University, YR President Jim Blythe has conducted a running battle against NSA's efforts to organize the campus. Sue Brown and Ann Miller of Mundelein have been active critics of NSA, as has been Kathy Stewart of Rosary. Loyola of Chicago disaffiliated a half dozen years ago, as did the University of Detroit. Northwestern has placed the group "on probation."

Schools which have dropped membership in recent months include USC, Clemson, Virginia, Brigham Young, Mary Baldwin College, Brooklyn College, Hope College, and West Virginia Wesleyan. At the University of Illinois, a special referendum found a majority of those voting in favor of disaffiliation. The effort to withdraw, however, foundered on a motion passed by the student senate, saying the referendum was of no effect unless fifty per cent of the entire student body voted. At DePauw, there has been a clamor to insure recognition of minority opinions within NSA. In addition, major efforts have been launched within the International Associated Women Students to bring about a critical inquiry into NSA's methods of operation.

A typical story of one conservative student's struggle within NSA is told by Stan Dempsey, a graduate of Colorado University. "In the spring of 1959," Dempsey recalls, "I was elected to the thirteen-man commission of the Associated Students of the University of Colorado. I was appointed by the President of the Student Body, at my request, to the post of Commissioner of NSA Affairs. Our first action was during the fall of 1959 meeting of the Rocky Mountain Region of NSA. At that time we prompted discussion groups to turn to the problems of NSA and ended up with a strongly worded resolution calling for NSA's leadership to work more on local student problems, such as abolition of the federal transportation tax for students, help with local campus problems, and more results for the individual students."

Dempsey's efforts met with little success. "My first approach to NSA," he concludes glumly, "was with the idea that enough action on the regional level might force a change in NSA. NSA's national leadership is too well entrenched for this."

Carol Bauman of Dunbarton College reported that, in spite of her school's active role in NSA, she found little evidence that student opinion was being channeled to the top echelons. "Last year," Mrs. Bauman wrote, "only three meetings were held, and the first of these was a 'planning' session. One assumes it took one whole session to plan for the other two." As for the contents of the two substantive meetings: "At the second meeting Harry Lunn, active Liberal Democrat student leader and former NSA president, addressed the group. The third meeting provided another opportunity for a Liberal plug, as Young Democrat leader Dick Murphy was given the floor. For the privilege of hearing these two Liberals, Dunbarton students paid regional and national dues to NSA, as well as about four hundred dollars for the expense of sending delegates to the student congress."

Perhaps the most telling and unremitting attack on NSA

has been launched by Kay Wonderlic. As Vice-President of the Student Senate, and as Northwestern's 1960 May Queen, Miss Wonderlic has wielded considerable influence on the campus. She has used it to put NSA into headlong flight.

Her principal area of concern has been with the structural flaws of NSA, and she has devoted considerable time to arguing that the group in fact "represents" little beyond the wishes of a few leaders. "Topics covered at the congress," she comments, "are not geared to current issues on member campuses, but to areas where NSA officers feel the campuses *should* be concerned. In other words, a few officers try to create interests for students with whose interests they are generally unfamiliar."

Although NSA has on occasion attempted to deny this and similar charges, its leaders have in effect confessed its truth. Robert Kiley, former NSA president, wrote in 1958: "If we are to hold to the thesis that college life contributes to the development of more intelligent citizenship, then we must assume that students *should be directed* to a greater social awareness."* NSA finds itself in a logical trap: it claims to speak in behalf of "more than a million students"—it is only the supposition that it represents the aggregate views of that many people that lends any weight to its pronouncements. Yet, according to Miss Wonderlic's testimony and Kiley's admission, the objective of NSA is to "direct," or to alter, students' opinions. The group cannot do both at the same time. It cannot simultaneously speak *to* and *for* that impressive one million.

Such bombardments from conservative students have drawn some critical attention to NSA from school administrations and from the press. In Kay Wonderlic's fight with NSA, Northwestern Dean James C. McLeod has said he was "four-square behind Kay's efforts to correct the evils that exist in the or-

* Italics added.

ganization." He added: "I think it is important that there be, if possible, a forum of voice for student opinion in the areas with which NSA concerns itself. But I feel that NSA has failed to reflect in any total way that which is the thinking of the modern American student." McLeod brought up another aspect of NSA. "We have had a great deal of difficulty," he said, "in getting a reliable roster of school membership. At no time has it been as large as they claim."

At Loyola, Dean Harry L. McCloskey said: "Loyola students who attended national conventions in the 1950s often reported parliamentary boondoggling in favor of the more leftist groups."

Miss Wonderlic is Chairman of an organization, consisting of both conservative and Liberal critics of NSA's internal structure, known as Students Committed to Accurate National Representation (640 Emerson St., Evanston, Illinois). Its objective is to establish that NSA, as presently constituted, does not represent American students, and to bring about changes in the NSA structure which will make it authentically representative. Among the various changes which SCANR advocates are:

1) Inclusion of minority reports (with twenty per cent approval) and vote tallies in NSA's book of policy statements. Currently, all statements appear as the unanimous opinion of all students.

2) All NSA public statements, both resolutions and in testimony by officials, should accurately note who is represented by such statements. Presently, even resolutions passed by the 35-member National Executive Committee are prefaced with, "In order to present the American student point of view . . ."

3) Change the preamble of the NSA constitution from "We, *the* students of the United States of America. . ." to "We, *as* students. . ."

4) Limit the power of the National Executive Committee to executive functions. It now passes legislation in the name of the entire association.

5) Prohibit committee chairmen from participating in debates without relinquishing the chair.

6) Give fair hearing to all sides of an issue by including all necessary and pertinent information in background and working papers, and in the selection of panel participants.

As an example of NSA's blatant rigging of meetings in favor of the Liberal position, SCANR cites a 1961 rally called to "examine" the Peace Corps. The delegates were told that "rather than a rally of student support, the conference will be a serious persual of all important aspects of the Peace Corps proposals." The facts in the matter, Miss Wonderlic says, were precisely the opposite:

Delegates found ample literature and 'working papers' which extolled the virtues of the Peace Corps in beautiful prose. Every major speaker at the conference, including Peace Corps director Sargent Shriver and . . . congressional supporters of the plan, was closely associated with the Corps and could not be expected to shed anything but a highly favorable light on the organization. Workshop chairmen, almost without exception, directed most of the discussion to persons favoring the Shriver-Kennedy version of the Peace Corps.

Moreover, urgency to "act" on the Peace Corps precluded any measured consideration of the issues involved. The delegates "were made to feel that their vote on the resolutions was more important than their careful consideration and discussion of them. Students who had come to learn and study were thrust into the unexpected position of having to legislate: to pass resolutions at any cost—including acting on some matters without bringing them to the floor for debate."

The Peace Corps rally provided, however, a significant skirmish between the student Liberals and the advancing young conservatives—on the Liberals' home grounds. Young Americans for Freedom, which has made surveillance of NSA one of its major projects, sent a group of delegates to the meeting at Washington's American University. Although vastly outnumbered by Peace Corps enthusiasts, the YAF delegates succeeded in making their influence felt, speaking from the floor in behalf of measures to convert the Corps from a charitable society to an effective weapon against Communism. Their views made a considerable splash in the papers, and conveyed to the public many of the glaring weaknesses of the Kennedy proposal. "The young conservatives," says YAF Chairman Robert Schuchman, "crowned their efforts by cajoling the conferees into modifying or changing at least half of the final resolutions."

Within NSA itself, the young conservatives have a long way to go. But they have made considerable progress in establishing that the group does not speak for American students as a whole. And NSA's high-handed tactics have helped inflame student ire on many campuses, putting added steam behind the youthful swing to the right.

IX

The Intellectuals

> ". . . in the field of economic and political phi-
> losophy there are not many who are influenced
> by new theories after they are twenty-five or
> thirty years of age, so that the ideas which civil
> servants and politicians and even agitators apply
> to current events are not likely to be the newest.
> But soon or late, it is ideas, not vested interests,
> which are dangerous for good or evil."
>
> J. M. KEYNES

THE CONSERVATIVE MOVEMENT has produced, not
merely picket-line enthusiasts and junior politicians, but a
high incidence of scholars and journalists. The young conservatives, by and large, are deeply interested in ideas, and
are capable of elaborating them with verbal power and dialec-
tical grace.

With so high a quota of intellectuals, the movement promises not only to endure, but to expand geometrically in days
to come. For the minds now being formed, now fusing a philosophy of man and government, will themselves be seminal influences upon still other minds. The movement is undergirded
not merely by youthful spirit, but by the lasting energy of ideas.

The sources of this intellectual renaissance are many, each

representing some recoil from the present orthodoxy, some search for alternatives. The movement can be reduced to its several components in many ways, depending upon the principle of identification. It reveals differences in philosophy, in perception of the crisis, in emphasis on appropriate lines of activity. Some groups reveal the influence of a particular intellectual leader; most pointedly, one rebellious professor or another will have profound effect upon the thinking of conservative students at his school. Particular schools, irrespective of the faculty, produce particular kinds of conservatives, with a style and tone all their own. For unexplained reasons, there will be a burst of conservative activity at some school or other where there has come together a notable concentration of bright young men, awakened to the ancient but ageless truths of conservatism. And finally, there have been a number of catalytic agents—schools, training programs, seminars—established to bring conservatives together, to impart certain essentials of the conservative philosophy, and to let them exchange ideas. All of these influences—men, schools, regions—have left a particular impress on the thinking of the students.

My comments are of course conditioned by what I have witnessed most closely, and this description should be so understood. On what I have observed, there have been two broad areas of conservative activity—each with its own regional emphasis and style. There has been a powerful burst of intellectual activity along the Eastern Seaboard, ranging from Harvard in the North to Virginia and the Carolinas in the South. In this flowering, a whole new school of young writers has appeared. Although they have been drawn from various parts of the country, their development, and the bulk of their work, has occurred in the East, particularly in Washington and New York.

The other broad area of activity has been the Midwest—or more exactly, the central plains extending into Oklahoma and Texas—where the primary emphasis has been on political activity. Broadly speaking, the young conservatives of the East, of Washington and New York, are writers. Those of the Midwest are politicians.

But the categories, by necessity, are not hard and fast. Both groups recognize that theirs is a common venture, and that the times demand both verbalizing and action; both clear thinking on principles, and precinct legwork to put them into practice. Thus the Eastern group has, so to speak, minored in politics. The young writers there have not only turned out numerous articles and publications canvassing the intellectual default of Liberalism; they have also been active in the Loyalty Oath movement, in Youth for Goldwater, in YAF, in the Young Republicans.

The young pols of the Midwest have similarly taken time from conventions and state and national elections to try their hand at the written word, and have succeeded quite well. In addition to bursts of literary achievement at Wisconsin and Chicago, a number of the most astute young politicians have demonstrated real capability as writers.

Just how many different pockets of intellectual activity have contributed to the revival is hard to say. In the field of economics, it is possible to identify some of the major sources. One particularly worth noting, because it reaches past the college level to students in the secondary grades, is the Bronx High School of Science. A group of bright young men at this New York school for the gifted became interested, in the early 1950s, in the teachings of Ludwig von Mises. From their studies of the free economy, they advanced into other areas of conservative thought. Many of them are now in the forefront of young conservative activities.

Mises and other conservative economists at NYU's School of Business Administration have been an important influence on many of the young conservatives. A second center of conservative teaching on economic matters is the University of Chicago. And the Department of Economics at Grove City College in Pennsylvania has had notable effect on a number of conservative students.

Also influential in shaping the views of the young people has been an institution known as the Freedom School, conducted by newspaper editor Robert LeFevre of Colorado Springs, Colorado. Purveying a brand of libertarian economics as pure as that of Mises, and sometimes more so, the Freedom School has helped form the careers of a number of young conservatives. The Freedom School describes its outlook as "the libertarian philosophy of individualism." That philosophy, it explains, holds "that man is by nature a free being. It is the concept enunciated by the founders of this American republic. It explains and endorses free enterprise and private ownership. It analyzes and exposes collectivism in its various guises." Among the student leaders who have passed through the Freedom School's portals are Edwin McDowell, David Franke, Roger Claus, Robert C. Adams, and Gale Pfund.

A parallel effort was ISI's summer school at Grove City College, described in Chapter III. Three similar schools were launched in the summer of 1961, by the Tuller Foundation for the Advancement of Economic Thought, held at Yale, C. W. Post College on Long Island, and Westminster Choir College. Young Americans for Freedom collaborated in staging these schools.

A principal reason for the concentration of these young people in Washington is yet another "school"—the journalistic workshop conducted by *Human Events,* from which fully a dozen conservative writers have emerged.

Some of this development clearly reflects regional differences. In the South, the young conservatives have exhibited principal concern with the tangle of political and philosophical questions involved in the question of segregation and states' rights. Midwesterners have found their way most readily into the ranks of the Republican Party, thanks to the GOP's historic conservatism there. The Eastern seaboard group has taken some of its tone from the prevailing styles in the Ivy League schools, in New York, and in Washington.

Finally, the influence of national conservative figures is clearly apparent: schools and subdivisions of conservative thought have aggregated around such writers as Ayn Rand, Mises, F. A. Hayek, Russell Kirk—and around such political figures as Senator Taft, Senator Goldwater, or Congressman Bruce Alger.

Out of all these influences has come a "new wave" of conservative writers capable of entering the lists against Liberalism, at both the senior and junior levels, and of doing competent ideological battle.

One of the most learned and eloquent of these is Garry Wills, who has just taken his Ph.D. at Yale (for a study of Heraclitus and Aeschylus). In addition to his scholarly pursuits, Wills has been a regular contributor to *National Review.* His writing is informed by a deep and extensive acquaintance with the literature, philosophy, and religious legacy of the West. At twenty-six, besides receiving his doctorate, he has already published a book *(Chesterton: Man and Mask),* taken a writing position with the Richmond *News Leader,* and moved on to a junior fellowship with the Institute of Hellenic Studies.

Wills' predecessor with the Richmond paper was Richard Whalen, also twenty-six, now an editorial writer for the *Wall Street Journal* and a frequent contributor to *National Review*. Whalen suggested the precocity of the right wing by nailing down the position of associate editor with the *News Leader* the day before his twenty-second birthday. Between Richmond and Wall Street, he also served a term as a contributing editor of *Time*.

Another brilliant young writer with a book to his credit— two in fact—is Roger Lea MacBride. MacBride, thirty-two, is a graduate of Princeton, where he did unremitting battle with the famous Professor H. H. Wilson. He also found time to write a lengthy research paper on the Electoral College, which was published by the Caxton Printers of Caldwell, Idaho. He later wrote a second book, *Treaties vs. The Constitution*, widely distributed during the dispute over the Bricker amendment. He has contributed to *National Review* and *The American Statesman*.

A third young scholar, Dr. Z. Michael Szaz of St. John's University, is the author of *Germany's Eastern Frontiers*, a study of the controversy over the Oder-Neisse provinces, and a compelling indictment of Western policy during and after World War II. Dr. Szaz, 31, is also editor-in-chief of a quarterly journal, *Free World Forum*.

In addition to Wills and Whalen, a number of conservative writers have been making their way into the newspaper world. One is 26-year-old Edwin McDowell, now an editorial writer for *The Arizona Republic*. McDowell, a graduate of Temple, is a former ISI student, and edited the McGraw-Edison Company's Public Affairs Newsletter before moving to Phoenix. Munro Roberts III, of Yale and Washington University, serves on the staff of the St. Louis *Globe-Democrat*. Roberts, twenty-five, attended the Sharon conference which founded YAF. He served a previous stint with the Los Angeles *Examiner*, and now has two novels in process of composition.

As is ordinarily the case in American letters, the South has been productive of young conservative writers. One distinguished product of the South, Robert Y. Drake, twenty-seven, has served on the faculty of Northwestern University, and contributed frequently to both *National Review* and *Modern Age*. In Louisiana, two youthful spokesmen for conservatism have assumed important editorial responsibilities. At the age of twenty-six, an articulate young conservative named Dallas Roper became managing editor of the *Monroe Morning World*, described by one prominent journalist as "the most important paper in the state after the New Orleans, Shreveport and Baton Rouge papers." Another conservative, 30-year-old Tom Kelly, has assumed the editorship of the daily paper in Jennings, Louisiana.

Nor is the conservative movement wanting for writers on the feminine side. Joan Didion, twenty-six, is an associate editor of *Vogue*, and a regular contributor to *National Review*. "I went to work for *Vogue*," she says, "because I had won a contest they used to run for college seniors—the Prix de Paris—the most notorious winner of which, predating me by five years, was Jacqueline Bouvier." Miss Didion is expert at digesting a smorgasbord of books into single luminous, entertaining review, and has become a standard contributor to the *National Review* literary department. She has two books of her own in the making, one of which is in the hands of Doubleday, the other as yet uncommitted.

Edith Kermit Roosevelt, thirty-one, granddaughter of Theodore Roosevelt, has carved out an independent reputation for herself by holding down a city room job with the Newark *Star-Ledger,* while simultaneously syndicating her own national column. Her weekly commentary on the news, vigorously conservative, is carried in some thirty newspapers.

Philippa Schuyler, twenty-eight, established a brilliant career as a concert pianist and composer, then went on to become an accomplished professional writer. Daughter of the famous Negro journalist, George Schuyler, she has travelled extensively in Africa, and has done considerable work as a foreign correspondent there. Her articles have been carried by the Spadea syndicate, *National Review,* the Manchester *Union-Leader* and other newspapers. She is the author of a book, *Adventures in Black and White.*

Carol Bauman, twenty-four, has also established a dual career. She is both a political activist (former Co-Chairman of the College Young Republicans, former Executive Secretary of College Youth for Nixon, currently legislative assistant to Congressman Donald Bruce), and a journalist of note. She has published articles in *The Individualist* and *National Review,* served as editor of the *Campus Republican* and on the editorial staff of the Young Republican *News.* She is currently Managing Editor of YAF's publication, *The New Guard.*

The editor-in-chief of *The New Guard* is Lee Edwards, twenty-nine, son of the Chicago *Tribune's* noted correspondent, Willard Edwards. Young Edwards has also served as Editor of the Young Republican *News* and published articles in *National Review* and *Human Events.* A graduate of Duke, he is currently employed as Press Aide to Senator John M. Butler of Maryland.

Among *The New Guard's* associate editors is C. Robert Ritchie, twenty-five, a graduate of George Washington University. Ritchie, a former News Editor of the YR *News,* just completed a stint as vice-chairman of the YR's publicity committee, and as editor of the group's national convention program. His writings have also appeared in *The Individualist* and *National Republic.*

Kenneth E. Thompson, twenty-six, also graces the editorial board of the YAF publication. Thompson, a graduate of Harvard and a founder of the conservative club there, experienced a meteoric rise at *Army Times,* where in a matter of months he ascended to the rank of associate editor. He has recently joined the staff of the Washington newsletter, *Human Events.*

All of the various conservative publications have contributed to the rise of these young writers, but *Human Events*—thanks to its unique journalism school—has unquestionably been the most productive. In addition to Thompson, there are several young writers now at work on the *Human Events* staff. Among its corps of Assistant Editors are Allan Ryskind, twenty-five, son of Morrie Ryskind, the playwright and newspaper columnist (in addition to his work for *Human Events,* young Ryskind has made several contributions to *National Review,* reflecting the same kind of humor that has made his father famous, and to *The New Guard*); George Fowler, twenty-six, formerly with the *New York Daily News,* a graduate of Columbia and one-time prize-fighter, also a contributor to *The New Guard;* John Benedict, thirty-three, a mainstay of the *Human Events* staff. Benedict, who handles the publication's voluminous reprint section, formerly served as editor of a weekly newspaper in Montgomery County, Maryland. *Human Events'* Business Manager is W. B. Hicks, Jr., twenty-nine, a graduate of Del Mar College in Corpus Christi, and a writer as well as a businessman. Hicks' writings have appeared both in *National Review* and *Human Events.*

Many graduates of the *Human Events* school have gone on

to other positions in conservative journalism. David Franke, twenty-three, who became Editorial Assistant for *National Review* (and whose other activities have been chronicled elsewhere in these pages), has also served as editor of various Young Republican journals and of ISI's publication, *The Individualist*. Antoni Gollan, also twenty-three, likewise began his journalistic career at *Human Events,* and went on to an editorial position at *National Review.* Still in college, Gollan is currently an editorial columnist for the Miami *Hurricane.* John Weicher, executive secretary of Youth for Goldwater, and an editor of a new conservative journal at the University of Chicago, worked for the Washington publication for a year after his graduation from Michigan. William C. Brady II, twenty-seven, currently vice-president of a group combatting Communism in the Caribbean, who helped launch the conservative counterattack at Harvard, went from his *Human Events* job to become legislative assistant to Congressman James Davis of Georgia; and Robert Goldsborough, thirty-one, now a research analyst for the House Committee on Un-American Activities, also did a tour of duty on the newsletter's editorial staff.

Yet another who apprenticed at *Human Events* is Douglas Caddy, 23-year-old National Director of Young Americans for Freedom. Caddy has published articles in *National Review, The Individualist,* and *USA* magazine. As a student at the Georgetown University School of Foreign Service, he edited the *Foreign Service Courier.* He succeeded Edwin McDowell as Editor of McGraw-Edison's Public Affairs newsletter.

Caddy's colleague, YAF Chairman Robert Schuchman, has proved himself a talented writer. A graduate of the Bronx High School of Science, Schuchman authored a hilarious spoof of the New Frontier, which was printed in *National Review, Insight and Outlook,* and several other publications. Currently enrolled at Yale Law School, he has also written for *The New Guard.* Other products of the Bronx school include William Schulz, George Riesman, and Ralph Raico. Schulz, one of the fastest-rising young conservative journalists, worked for a year with *Human Events,* and for two years with Fulton Lewis, Jr. Now twenty-two, he has placed articles with *National Review, Human Events,* and *The New Guard,* and has written for several metropolitan newspapers.

Riesman has served as a member of the faculty at the City College of New York. In addition to his pedagogical duties, administered at the age of twenty-six, he has contributed a withering analysis of J. Kenneth Galbraith's notions of "affluence" to *Human Events.* Raico, twenty-four, received his BA degree from CCNY in 1959. He is presently enrolled at the University of Chicago, studying with the Committee on Social Thought, and serving as editor-in-chief of the *New Individualist Review.* He has been published in *The Freeman.*

Many of these young conservatives have, as I have noted, written for *National Review.* Others in their mid-twenties who have appeared in its pages are J. D. Futch and John Leonard, both of whom contributed, in 1959, to the magazine's special "youth" issue and who appear frequently in its book review section. Another youthful *National Review* regular is Peter Crumpet, who lives and writes in Spain. And Daniel Mahoney, a young New York lawyer, has been published in both *National Review* and *Modern Age.*

Many of these young people—Schulz, Gollan, Franke, Weicher—are still on campus. There are many others like them, and the number of young conservative journalists promises to increase spectacularly in the years ahead.

Miss Annette Courtemanche of Molloy College has been a regular contributor to the *Crosier,* her school paper. She has also contributed articles to the Brooklyn *Tablet*. At Princeton, James B. Burnham, son of *National Review's* senior editor, has been for the last two years a regular columnist for the *Princetonian*. At Monmouth College in Illinois, conservative leader Roberta Egan is a regular columnist for the Monmouth *Oracle*. At Shelton College in New Jersey, young conservatives Carl T. McIntire and Deborah Steele served as Co-Editors of the *Skylander,* the undergraduate newspaper. At Yale University, Mike Uhlmann, head of the Calliopean Society, is Vice Chairman of the *News,* and does a regular editorial page column. At DePauw University, Greg Copeland, head of the Conservative Club, has served as a regular columnist for the school paper (he has also worked on the Dayton, Ohio, *Journal-Herald*) and Miss Anne Husted is one of the paper's principal editors. At William and Mary, the student newspaper has been under the stewardship of conservatives Al Volkmann and Allan Brownfeld. And the undergraduate writers branch out; Marquette law student Peter Wheeler Reiss is the author of a pamphlet, "Why We Are Losing the Third World War," which has been widely reprinted and inserted in the *Congressional Record*; William Ackerman of Iowa wrote a searching critique of an economics text which attracted the attention of *The Wall Street Journal* and kicked up a national controversy.

A center of literary activity has been the University of Wisconsin—long a hotbed of "progressivist" ideas. Wisconsin was the site of the first sustained publication of an undergraduate conservative journal—*Insight and Outlook,* which was the brainchild of Alan McCone, a young writer and organizer who launched the Wisconsin Conservative Club, with the help of ISI, in 1957. The magazine dumbfounded Wisconsin Liberals. "From out of the land of LaFollette," commented one undergraduate magazine, "believe it or not, comes this reactionary magazine, honest to God. It has always seemed to us that the college campus was just not the place for reactionaries."

But whatever the case for "reactionaries," the Wisconsin campus proved to be just the place for *Insight and Outlook,* now in its fourth year of publication. Shining star of the magazine for the past two years has been a formidable young man named Richard S. Wheeler. Wheeler, twenty-six, did a stint of commercial writing in Los Angeles before returning to his home state to enroll at Wisconsin University. As a regular columnist for the *Daily Cardinal,* he established himself as the campus *enfant terrible.* By his junior year, he had become executive editor of *Insight and Outlook,* a post from which he regularly flayed Liberals, both local and national, with Menckenesque disdain. On the basis of his showing at Wisconsin, we shall all be hearing much more of Dick Wheeler in years to come.

Insight and Outlook itself is a lively, twenty-page monthly magazine, carrying a heavy quota of advertising from local merchants. Its 1960-61 editor was Gale Pfund, a scholarly young man of twenty-one, who attended Bob LeFevre's Freedom School in Colorado. Roger Claus, twenty-three, McCone's successor as head of the Conservative Club, has also been a steady contributor, as have Associate Editors Tony Cadden and Millard Johnson.

Insight and Outlook was the pilot venture in what has become a growing move toward conservative publications on the campus. At the University of Chicago, a group of ISI students have begun to publish a magazine as notable for its range and philosophic depth as is *Insight and Outlook* for its verve and audacity. Entitled *New Individualist Review,* the Chicago journal is a bimonthly canvass of the conservative effort, covering aspects from the most recondite to the most immediate. Its first issue, attractively printed and laid out, featured an article by Professor Milton Friedman, concerning the vital nexus between capitalism and political liberty (reprinted in *The Wall Street Journal*); a critique of progressive education by Robert Schuettinger; a prospectus for the Republican Party by John Weicher; a biographical essay on the German naturalist and philosopher, Baron von Humboldt, by Ralph Raico; a plea for the restoration of value by John P. McCarthy; and a deft analysis of F. A. Hayek's "concept of freedom," by Ronald Hamowy.

These articles are like nothing seen on most college campuses. Founded in a clear perception of the modern crisis, and executed with verbal strength and clarity, *New Individualist Review*, I imagine, was as great a shock to Chicago Liberals as *Insight and Outlook* was to their counterparts at Wisconsin.

At the University of Pennsylvania, a third ISI affiliate, the Eleutherian Society, has brought out its own publication, *Analysis*—so named in honor of Frank Chodorov's journal of the 1940s. *Analysis,* edited by Penn sophomores Richard Lee Huff and William Henry Regnery, began in April 1961 with a barrage of articles by undergraduates, faculty members and guest writers. In its manifesto of purpose, *Analysis* said:

We will endeavor to effect a change in the thinking of the students and faculty of the University of Pennsylvania to a more conservative outlook.

We will oppose more government control over the life of the individual and will, in most cases, seek to remove governmental influences.

We will oppose the forces of international and internal Communism which we believe are now the greatest single threat to our liberties.

We will emphasize victory over the Communist ideology rather than mere coexistence with it.

We will defend the Constitution of the United States and attempt to see that it is not perverted by anyone, whether he be in the legislature, the courts, or the executive. . . .

Finally, we will support the idea that the individual is the keystone of society; that each individual is unique in his own way; and that arbitrary force unjustly violates the concept of free will, and if applied long enough and widely enough, will destroy our civilization.

The response of the Pennsylvania community to those uncompromising sentiments may well be imagined.

In Jackson, Mississippi, students have brought out a monthly newspaper called *The Campus Conservative,* which proclaims the rise of conservatism among Southern collegians. A publication by the same name is produced at the University of Miami, edited by Andy Gollan, Steve Slepin, and Michael Thompson. At Ohio State, there is a conservative journal called *Proponent.* At Grove City, conservative students publish *The Entrepreneur,* a newsletter devoted to a defense of the free enterprise system, financed by bulk sales to local businessmen. At Tulane, students Haywood Hillyer, John Eckland, and Richard Regan publish *Liberator*—a magazine which, in format and content, is a competent analogue to *National Review.*

Thus, at this writing, the conservative movement can claim no less than eleven publications written and produced by young people: *The Gentlemen of the Right, Insight and Outlook, New Individualist Review, Analysis,* two versions of *The Campus Conservative, Proponent, The Entrepreneur, Liberator, The Individualist,* and *The New Guard.* And as the various local publications are circulated nationally, students on other campuses begin to catch the spark of enthusiasm. It is safe to predict that in the years ahead many another conservative magazine will be born on American campuses.

What are the predominant intellectual concerns of these

young writers and editors? Some, I think, have been suggested in earlier chapters, by fragmentary quotations from various student leaders, from the Sharon Statement, from Youth for Goldwater manifestoes, from the ISI credo stated by Vic Milione. In general, the young conservatives represent the converse of the Liberal conformity. Whereas the present orthodoxy is permissive and statist, the young conservatives tend to be moralists and libertarians. Just as Liberalism unites compulsion with a plastic morality, so these conservatives seek to unite individual freedom with critical discipline. At the secular level, they have divided their concern between the global advance of Communism, with its fifth column in the United States, and the expanding domestic state. They are fervent anti-Communists in matters of foreign policy and internal security, and proponents of limited government in matters of domestic economy.

It is sometimes said that this constellation of beliefs is eclectic and inconsistent—a random gathering of mood and opinion rather than a coherent philosophy. Indeed, it is averred that the young conservatives' accent on personal freedom and limited government unfits them for the name "conservative." These young people, say their critics, are in reality classical liberals, and should call themselves such.

The doctrines of classical liberalism, pejoratively construed, are materialist and essentially amoral. They consist in reverence for economics, and the justification of freedom on the grounds that it is productive of material benefits. In their pure form, they tend to be relativist, rejecting the possibility of authority beyond the individual. Is this, in fact, the philosophy of the modern conservative movement?

To get some kind of answer to that question, I wrote to a number of young conservative leaders, and asked them to sketch a paragraph or so for me concerning their personal philosophies. I was agreeably surprised at the result—not only by the substantive content of the letters I received, but by the evidence of independent thought they suggested. I think I can best illumine the matter by letting these young people speak for themselves. Here are some sample replies:

Men cannot successfully follow the pragmatic practice of basing their policies on what seems to be expedient at the time; they must realize that there is a universal order of things, a moral law which cannot be flouted.

Anne Husted, DePauw University

I believe in original sin, and hold that man is both good and evil; that he cannot rely on reason alone, but must also rely on the wisdom of his ancestors, i.e., tradition. I believe in mixed government, as outlined in the Federal Constitution, which was the Burkean type of conservatism championed by John Adams and Madison.

I regard economics as a science or means, rather than a religion or philosophy. I favor the free enterprise system but not with the doctrinaire fervor of a libertarian.

C. Robert Ritchie, Associate Editor
The New Guard

I believe that man's ultimate destiny of union with God in the Beatific Vision is his most important consideration. Therefore any philosophy, to be tenable and true, must take into consideration what man is and what his destiny is. I find that politically, conservatism with its emphasis on the individual exercising his freedom while respecting the rights and freedom of his fellow men is the only position which I can hold and still be faithful to my basic premises, philosophically and theologically.

Carol Ann Nevin, University of Maryland

I consider myself a conservative; one who accepts natural law and the lessons of history as the guides to judgment in matters political, social, philosophical, and religious. To me, history and the natural law reveal that the family must be the cornerstone of society, and that the protection of individual and family rights is the principal duty of the state. Applying this philosophy to our modern age, I resist the intrusion of the state into areas which properly are the concern of the individual, alone or in voluntary cooperation with other persons; and I affirm that the government of the United States should apply itself instead to its legitimate concern—the protection of the just interests of our country and its citizens, and defense against all enemies, foreign and domestic.

David Franke, Young Americans for Freedom

... human nature ... requires political authority. But this authority has limitations based upon a Divine transcendence. The state is not absolute—it is not a be-all and end-all. Moreover, the political authority must be developed in accordance with man's nature; it cannot properly function as a medium for effecting wild-eyed programs that someone considers 'ideal' ... It is the tragedy of our times that today's political and social institutions are dominated by positivism, relativism, and historicism.

William R. Mapother, University of Virginia

Stable value, "the good," is more important than freedom, for it is the only thing (the only lasting thing) that makes freedom possible. Once "the good" has been established (embodied in a customary law and community tradition), as it has to its highest degree in the Western tradition, man's primary concern *is* freedom, first for its own sake and incidentally but powerfully for its explosively productive results (in all areas: economics, art, and science). The present erosion of Western traditional values hence deserves more than the present concern from conservatives, since any victory over the mechanics of collectivist government will be hollow and the result unstable if the essence of the West is not re-established.

Jameson G. Campaigne, Jr., Williams College

My first faith is in a higher order of things which I believe in the end must govern all human action. As imperfect persons, our moral obligation is to act in accordance with that higher order, and not to attempt to supplant it with an order of our own, which, being human, will by nature be imperfect and bad. Extending this philosophy, my second faith is in the ability of the individual to interpret the higher order and to act roughly in accordance with it and thus solve his own problems;

that no individual is innately qualified to rule over other men.
John W. Kolbe, Northwestern

The only basis of respect for the integrity of the individuality of the person and for the overriding value of his freedom is a belief in an organic moral order. Man's pursuit of virtue and the fulfillment of his duty to the moral order can be realized only in a political and economic condition of freedom. In the moral realm freedom is only a means whereby man can properly pursue his end which is virtue, and in the political realm freedom is the primary end.
Douglas C. Williams, Jr., Earlham College

My idea of conservatism arises from a belief in an absolute moral law which cannot be tested by scientific and epistemological questions. This law is a natural law of order given by God, and only to be recognized by man. Upon this law should the political order be founded. As far as we have discovered, this order is one in which government should *only* maintain a social and political condition, i.e., external defense, internal order, and a homogeneous system of justice, in which individuals may live their lives based on their own thinking and deciding—the freedom required for morality. Consequently the criterion by which conservatives test government is how much freedom it will afford, which is little or no government in areas other than defense, justice, and internal order.
Paul V. Niemeyer, Kenyon College

The ethical tendency of these statements, I think, is clearly opposed to the species of "classical liberalism" paraphrased above. Overwhelmingly, the students and youth leaders responding to my letter premised their regard for freedom upon an affirmation of a transcendent structure of morality. Moreover, while none has reasoned his case so tightly that professional philosophers could not pick flaws in it, I think these statements represent intellectual power of a high order. These students have approached the desideratum of Burke, tempering together "these opposite elements of liberty and restraint in one consistent work."

One final statement, from Michael Uhlmann of Yale University, sums up this position quite well. His own conservatism, Uhlmann writes, is Burkean in conception, premised upon "absolute standards of morality and of natural law, from which, in turn, the concept of the dignity and worth of the human being is derived." And he adds: "It is silly to speak of any type of morality unless man is a free agent, and thus the highest *political* goal becomes the preservation of individual liberties."

I do not mean to suggest that some of the students involved in the present uprising are not "classical liberals." There are some such, who may be traced, in large part, to the group of young people that appeared at the Bronx High School of Science in the early 1950s. These students were greatly influenced by Ludwig von Mises, whose seminars at New York University they audited with precocious regularity. With the advent of *Atlas Shrugged*, a number of them enlisted under the banner of Ayn Rand's "objectivism," a rationalist philosophy which elevates self-interest to the cardinal principle of life and which is explicitly anti-religious. The Randian ethic supplied a morality which these libertarians deemed congruent with Mises' economics, and so supplied them with a fully-rounded philosophy of laissez-faire existence. On the basis of the letters I received, however, this group represents only a fraction of the conservative revival. Most of the students begin their critique of Liberalism, not from economics, but from religious and philosophic conviction.

Granted that these students and their conservative allies are, philosophically, at swords'-points; for the present, the two groups have certain overriding interests in common, and for that reason have fused into a single movement. Once the proximate causes of alliance—the manifold difficulties attendant upon collectivist Liberalism—are dealt with, the classical liberals and the traditionalists may resume their ancient dialogue. But that day is a long way hence, and until then these two schools will labor side by side to dispose of a common enemy.

If I may sum up, then, the views expressed by most of the students with whom I have talked and corresponded, I should offer the following as a consensus:

1. The young conservative believes the central failing of Liberalism is its rejection of the greatest truth of the West: That ours is a universe ruled by God, Whose laws of faith and of ethical behavior should govern all aspects of human life. The Liberal, characteristically, is a relativist, who believes there are no absolutes. The conservative's first task is to affirm the primacy of God and the moral order of the universe; to establish that our lives are ruled by unchanging truths.

2. The young conservative believes that one injunction of the moral order, disregarded by collectivist Liberalism, is that no man has a discretionary commission to coerce another. Because the principal end of man is to shape his volition to the will of God, no man is empowered to distort or oppress another's will. The conservative thus exhibits a powerful concern for freedom, as the political context of moral choice. He believes that violation of freedom is a violation of personality, an intrusion upon the sacred contract between man and his Creator.

3. As a reflection of his concern for freedom, the conservative has taken up the case for the market economy. He finds that man's freedom is being leached away through the instrumentality of the state, intruding upon economic life. He finds that spurious simulacra of "economics" are used to sanction this process. At the scientific level, he finds the means of combating these false theories in Mises, Hayek, Roepke, Friedman.

4. In his concern to preserve the conditions of choice, the conservative is a Constitutionalist. He believes that the only

provable guarantee of freedom is the diffusion and limitation of power, as set forward in the Constitution of the United States. He perceives that the tripartite division of the federal government, and the reserved powers of the states, are the chief instruments by which this diffusion has been achieved in the United States. He is therefore an advocate of a limited executive and of judicial review, while at the same time believing that, in the logic of the federal equilibrium, the judiciary itself must be subject to restraint.

5. Finally, in his concern for freedom, he recognizes that the paramount danger facing the United States is the threat of international Communism. He perceives that Liberal methods for dealing with Communism have failed, and failed repeatedly. He believes the nature of the adversary is such that we cannot "coexist" with it, but must defeat it, if we are to survive.

Upon review, then, it appears that the principal object of the young conservatives is the affirmation of a transcendent moral order, and recognition of man's appropriate place in that order. The great secular concern received from that order is a regard for human freedom, and the integrity of human personality. These are the central positions. Those remaining—a program of economics, strict constitutionalism, vigorous anti-Communism—are in reality technical elaborations of these primary concerns. The young conservative may be, and generally is, a moralist, a libertarian, a free-market economist, a states' righter, an advocate of "congressional autonomy," a republican, and an anti-Communist, consecutively and simultaneously. These attitudes are not random fusions of contradictory or irrelevant moods; they are coherent aspects of a fundamental view of man and his nature, articulated in terms of the present crisis.

There is a final point to be covered. Throughout this discussion, I have emphasized the activism and the political energy of the young conservatives. This fact is frequently noted by those who seek to challenge its credentials as truly "conservative." Picket lines, giant rallies, lobbying, precinct work—these, it is objected, are not the stigmata of conservatism.

Such young people want to change everything—to dismantle "social gains"; in addition to favoring individualist goals, they want to use radical means. If they were truly "conservative," say their detractors, they would be content to accept the status quo—to rest with the "gains" legislated by the New Deal and its Democratic and Republican successors.

In this view, a conservative is complaisant, withdrawn, inclined to introspection. In his political preferences, he favors government by an "elite," and he likes to see society subdivided into hierarchies, with minimum opportunity for individual mobility. And, above all, the conservative is opposed to change. None of which consorts very well with the present shape of young conservative activity.

Before examining this criticism, I must acknowledge that its empirical foundation is sound: the young conservative of today *is* (1) determined upon change; (2) devoted to the cause of freedom; and (3) sometimes prone to use "radical" means. But do these things indicate that he is not a conservative?

The answer, of course, depends upon what one means by the word. If "conservatism" is an immutable catalogue of foibles, defining style of dress, views on personal activism, and political temperament, then today's young rebels are indeed not "conservative." For in these matters they often exhibit no continuity with the conservatives who have gone before them.

But if "conservatism" means, as I believe it should, a view of man, society, and the moral order; if it means philosophical convictions, rather than surface characteristics, then today's young rebels are, for the most part, true conservatives, and represent an authentic continuity with the great ideas of the conservative past.

Conservatism, as I conceive it, is not *primarily* a matter of mood and temperament—although it cannot be denied that certain matters of tone and style are, all other things being equal, more consonant with conservative principles than certain others. But conservatism is first and foremost a set of principles, a way of looking at man and his universe. And the other things are not equal.

There are two points of philosophy which have, through the ages, characterized the conservative. The first is the belief that ours is an ordered universe, informed by the purpose of a Divine Being. The second is that man, in seeking his place in this universe, is hampered by an imperfect mind and a vagrant will. Upon those postulates, the conservative constructs a view of society, of man's place in it, and of the institutions suitable to man. Because of them, he has favored a regime of stability premised upon a community of volition, and has tended to mistrust the unbridled exercise of power. Circumstances may change, but principles do not. In determining the political style appropriate to the conservative, the key question becomes: Are the circumstances congenial to the principles? As the answer varies, so must one's assessment of the methods by which circumstances may be accommodated, the principles sustained.

In general, we may assume that the conservative will resist change during periods in which the values he cherishes predominate. Since these values have, by and large, been the basis of Western civilization, the conservative has become habituated to quiescence—to preserving and nurturing the existent order. As certain changes occur, he strikes an intuitive balance: So

long as the main tradition is preserved, he is willing to accommodate the change. Every tradition must provide latitude for
adjustment; this fact, plus the conservative's habituation to a
general continuity in his institutions, makes him willing to
accept changes of degree, and unwilling to resort to "radical"
methods to overturn those changes, once established. Well and
good. But there comes a point where changes in degree fuse into
a change in *kind:* where the essential tradition is not amended,
or modified, but violated; when the changes enacted are no
longer adjustments which allow the central principles to survive in altered circumstances, but revolutionary acts conspiring
to deny those principles. Faced with such conditions, the conservative's characteristic mood no longer avails. By acquiescing
in the established subversion of its principles, that mood becomes a silent partner in the work of destruction. The conservative must then consider what techniques are available to
him, within the moral universe he cherishes, to restore his tradition.

It is just such a condition which today prevails in America,
indeed throughout the West, and it is just such a condition
which confronts the young man or woman who, grasping the
essential lessons of our tradition, decides that he or she is a conservative. Frank S. Meyer, writing in *Modern Age,* notes that
in our era "a revolutionary force" has shattered "the unity and
balance of civilization." In such an era, he says, conservatism

. . . cannot be limited to that uncritical acceptance, that uncomplicated reverence, which is the essence of natural conservatism. The world of idea and symbol and image has been
turned topsy-turvy; the life-stream of civilization has been cut
off and dispersed.

Meyer concludes that a *conscious* conservatism is required, a
conservatism which will "select and adjudge." Thus, compelled

by his altered circumstances, the young conservative is led to break with the "natural piety" which is most congenial to the conservative temperament. He is required to be, in the non-pejorative sense, an ideologue—with clearly conceived notions of how principles and institutions and men affect one another to form a culture and a society within it.

If that much is granted, the alleged "radicalism" of today's young conservatives becomes comprehensible. Confronted with an established revolution, the conservative must seek to *change* the status quo; he has no other means of affirming his tradition. And in seeking that alteration, he must invoke certain of the techniques which are effective in producing change.

X

The Conservative Future

"Mere unassisted merit advances slowly, if—what
is not very common—it advances at all."

SAMUEL JOHNSON

THE ACADEMY IS NO LONGER a comfortable fiefdom of
the left; it has become instead what it ought to be, a battleground of ideas. But these advances are only a beginning—a
beachhead. Although the conservative movement has had its
impact on campus politics, it has a long way to go before it
reaches parity with the opposition. The *dominant* element on
American campuses, on my observation and on the basis of voluminous statistical evidence, is still Liberalism.

Given their own permissive ideology, the Liberals may tolerate, even welcome, the renewed burst of conservatism, if only
because it makes life more interesting. But that tolerance has
its boundaries, which are soon reached when it becomes apparent that the conservative challenge is more than a pro forma
statement of alternatives. The Liberal conformity has, after all,
a vast apparatus of power at its command, and we may expect
that apparatus to be put to good use. A few examples have
already been touched upon; several others are mentioned in

the Epilogue which follows. Whether other similar episodes
will ensue depends, to a considerable extent, upon the condition of the Liberal conscience, and upon the conservatives'
ability to illuminate such matters against the backdrop of Liberalism's own stated values.

The point of these reflections is that there is nothing inevitable about the rise and fall of ideologies. The "swing of the
pendulum" to which the conservative revival is usually as-
cribed is only partially that; the pendulum does not swing of
its own momentum; someone has to push it. It is perhaps ob-
ligatory that young people of independent mind seek out alternatives to an airless orthodoxy; but there is no discoverable
law of nature which says the impulse to resistance will issue in
success. When counterpressures are brought to bear, that impulse can, if unfortified, falter and subside.

The conservative movement among American youth has
reached its present eminence through sustained effort by men
and women who believe in its principles, and who have pros-
elytized in its behalf. Because they made the conservative alternative available to the students, the urge to resist encountered
the theoretical substance of conservatism, united it with the
value precepts inculcated in the home, and became articulate.
Misgivings became audible dissent, and conveyed to others the
possibility of open resistance. By this affective movement, dis-
parate impulses became joined in the crucible of rebellion.

If the conservative movement is to prosper, it must not assume
that success will simply happen to it; its participants and its
patrons must continue the kind of work that has brought it this
far. "History" will not do it for them.

But even if we assume such effort to be forthcoming, the
conservative movement has certain other tests which it must
meet if it is to succeed. These have principally to do with the

form and the stress of its activities: the way in which it seeks to
engage reality, and to shape its hard substance to the contours
of principle. They involve the tone and style of the movement,
the proximate objectives it seeks or should seek, and the degree
to which it should restrain conviction in the interest of *Real-
politik*. All of these questions have been suggested by one or
another of the young conservatives themselves. For, in addition to their exuberance and enthusiasm, these young people
express a mature and intelligent concern for the future of the
movement; they exhibit the kind of self-critical awareness
which—distinguished from the paralysis imposed by self-doubt
in fundamental matters—can refine and strengthen their common enterprise. They are alert to weakness and fallacy, even
in their own camp, and are concerned to insure that the conservative effort is neither dissipated in frivolity nor isolated in
fanaticism.

First and foremost, the young conservatives are anxious that
their ranks consist of those who understand the philosophy of
conservatism, and are not simply, in the words of Bob Lucock
of Grove City, "irresponsible children bandstanding from platform to platform" (which he believes most of them are not).
"The whole movement," comments Frank Blatchford of Cornell, "is as worthless as a hollow piece of clay if its supporters
do not think for themselves." And Bill Dennis of Earlham says:

I am scared of a swiftly growing conservative movement. . . .
It will attract people who are not really committed to the conservative philosophy. I once heard a young conservative who
was far more versed in politics and economics than I say, 'I am
a conservative in everything but in social morals and philosophy.' None of us can live our ideals, but simply to disregard
them leaves us with a staleness and expediency long since the
ally of every act of oppression and intolerance the world has
ever known. This, I feel, is a clear and present danger.

Other reflections in a similarly thoughtful vein, concerned to keep conservatism faithful to its heritage, come from young men like Paul Niemeyer of Kenyon, Lee Edwards of YAF, Dick Whalen of *The Wall Street Journal*. Misgivings on other points are expressed by such people as Donald Micken, first president of Montana State's Conservative Club, and by Brice Oakley, 1960-61 Chairman of the College Young Republicans of Iowa.

The common theme of these remarks has to do with the future of the conservative movement: Will it become cheapened and diluted in an effort to become a mass phenomenon? Or will it become so perfectionist in intent that it will fail to achieve any sort of tangible results?

As at the senior level, there are two schools of thought among the young conservatives—the "purists" and the "realists." The purist school holds that conservatives must never seek to accommodate their principles to existing conditions; it insists that conservatism must propound its unalloyed doctrine in all circumstances. If it is rejected by society, they say, so much the worse for society.

The realists argue that we must forget the nonsense of insisting upon principle, and tack with the prevailing winds. We must understand, they argue, that we are confronted with a condition, not a theory, and bend ideology to the demands of a bad situation.

The purist school, in general, anticipates a total debacle before things get better, hoping a remnant of the faithful will rise from the debris and restore our institutions. The realists tend to wage a delaying action: to soften the impact of the Liberal advance, fight a day-to-day battle, and hope the result is sufficiently nondescript to preserve at least some of our freedoms.

Which road should the young conservatives choose? In answering that question they are confronted with a difficult choice: If they cast their lot with the purists, a debacle may indeed overtake us—and there may be no resurrection from its ashes. And if they opt for realism, they may find they have lost the battle anyway, through the surrender of their ideals.

My own belief is that the young conservative is confronted with a dual assignment: He must hold to the ideology and the ultimate objectives of the purists; yet he must work in the daily political struggle to achieve realist objectives. If he has the qualities of mind and will which characterize the successful revolutionist, he will be able to achieve both. Indeed, in proper modulation, purism and realism subserve and strengthen one another. The deep commitment of the "true believer" energizes a movement and induces its members to perform the labor of effective politics. And the immediate tasks of politics— the battles for the loyalty oath, for the soul of the Republican Party, against federal aid and the diminution of national sovereignty—maintain the pockets of freedom in which the processes of regeneration can do their work.

Thanks to its ideological clarity, the conservative movement today has certain assets which it did not have ten years ago— principally a group of young spokesmen who can carry its message to the country, who have the stamina for rigorous endeavor, and who can shape still other minds in the years ahead. These tasks cannot be well performed by those who have muddled their understanding, or compromised their commitment. Those who would surrender conviction for ambiguous victories should recall that creeds and systems flourish accordingly as their adherents believe deeply in them and work to make them succeed. The achievements of ISI, YAF, the conservative swing of the Young Republicans—these have happened because committed and capable people worked to make them happen.

The daily battles of conservative vs. Liberal should be fought, and vigorously. But they should be understood, I think, *sub specie aeternitatis,* as a holding action. They will achieve no overnight successes, and they cannot be an end in themselves. Those who set their sights on immediate results are likely to suffer the bitter disappointment which enervates and demoralizes. True, certain early satisfactions are possible— and they should not be disparaged. Thanks to the activities of the young conservatives, the entire spectrum of campus politics has been moved somewhat to the right. From the conservative point of view, this alteration is gratifying; but it is not, and cannot be, the major focus of conservative effort. The present generation has been subjected to predominantly Liberal teachings; it must, in the aggregate, end up by being a predominantly Liberal generation.

The important generation is that which follows, and which will be tutored by this one. If the conservative effort of today is expanded, but kept faithful to principle, it will continue to draw to its standard the "character elite," the kind of young people I have described in the preceding chapter. This elite, in turn, will set the prevailing style of the intellectual journals, the pedagogy, and the mass media twenty-five years hence. And those influences will train the succeeding generation. If the conservative effort is carried through to that denouement, it will have succeeded in making the country conservative.

This conclusion is, I think, the common one of the young conservatives themselves. The conservative effort, observes Dick Wheeler of Wisconsin, is not "to preach," but "to set examples for the rest to follow." The movement, says Tom Huston, has not yet reached the mass of the students, but consists of "a hard core of leaders who are good scholars and articulate spokesmen. . . ." For both reasons, the young rebels, while desirous of practical results, are wary of playing their hand too early, or of abandoning their ideals for a pyrrhic victory at the polls. "Conservatives should not attempt to gain the presidency in 1964," says Greg Copeland of DePauw, "if it means they will have to make extensive concessions to the Liberals in order to do it." The objective, after all, is not to control society, through the machinery of politics, but to change it, through a redirection of values. Yale's Mike Uhlmann observes that we might elect a Goldwater, but asks, "how do we erase thirty years of the bureaucratic mentality?"

Immediate victories should be gained, these young people believe, in every possible arena, but not at the price of forfeiting principle. The ultimate goal must be a final and lasting victory, and for that objective only the power of conviction will suffice. "It will take several years of foundation-laying before the program we all want can be built to endure the test of time," writes Dave Coldren of Antioch. And until that foundation is established, the young conservatives will fight it out as best they can, while keeping their eyes fixed on the future.

The road they have chosen is a long one, requiring the divergent abilities to hold a long-range goal in view, and to wage sometimes intensive struggles on issues of the moment. It is a program calling for considerable effort, and it depends for its success on the intellectual and moral qualities of those called upon to achieve it.

The ultimate resource of the conservative movement, then, is characterological: It requires men of strong conviction to wage this sort of patient struggle—the very sort of men who can attract and persuade the generation which follows. In proportion as conservatism can produce such leaders, and as they are annealed in the fires of combat, will the movement achieve its objectives. On the present showing, it has been remarkably successful. With continued effort, it can become more so.

EPILOGUE
Academic Freedom: In Theory, and in Practice

"Until recently the chief function of the sophisticated, the priests and the scribes, has been to stabilize custom and validate social authority by perpetuating the tradition and interpreting it in a manner conformable to the understanding of common man. During the last three hundred years . . . there has emerged a new class of learned men, successors to the priests and scribes, whose function is to increase rather than to preserve knowledge, to undermine rather than to stabilize custom and social authority."

CARL BECKER

I

Who Rules in the Academy?

IN ASSESSING THE CONSERVATIVE REVIVAL on the campus, and the conditions which have nourished it, we must attend to the issue of "academic freedom." For it is in this guise that Liberal doctrine has, over the years, been implanted in the minds of American students, and it is the abuses committed in its name which have inflamed conservative ire. "Academic freedom," roughly and in theory, means free inquiry, with a hearing given to all alternatives. It should be the conservative's task to determine if free inquiry is what we in fact have on the campus, and whether it is what we want there.

It has been suggested in the opening pages of this book that the "conformity" possessing the United States is Liberalism, and that it is particularly prevalent on the college campus. Before erecting any theories on that affirmation, I think it wise to elaborate upon it further.

The findings of presumably disinterested observers suggest that our conformity, if we examine it carefully, reveals two principal characteristics. The first is that, in the realm of value, the "other-directed" ethic is *permissive;* that is, it provides no fixed standards of loyalty; other-directed people are not interested in right and wrong, but in getting along. The second

is that the other-directed ethic is *statist;* people with no internalized code of values must turn outward for guidance. They
tend to mimic their contemporaries, and yearn to submerge
themselves in the collectivity.

Is this conformity, as I have suggested, prevalent on American campuses? How "permissive," for example, are American
faculties, and how permissive have they made the students over
whom they exercise so precious a stewardship? "Permissiveness," or tolerance, may proceed from any one of a number
of sources—compassion, ennui, ignorance, confusion. As described by Riesman, it is generally associated with a loss of
inner conviction; other-directed people are tolerant because
they have no firm opinions about anything. That mood of
ethical indifference has been fostered by a number of influences
in American thought, and has been variously urged under the
rubric of nominalism, positivism, pragmatism. The generic
term for such attitudes is "relativist." Their common characteristic is the rejection of general propositions which are morally binding.

Conservatives tend, with some reason if not with total accuracy, to group these attitudes under the heading of "atheism"
or "agnosticism." Systems of belief which affirm certain immutable moral laws are most commonly designated as "religions"
—although there are of course some moral systems, usually constructed by philosophers, which are not explicitly religious
(i.e., which accept certain generalizations but claim no supernatural sanctions for them). Thus a consistently anti-religious
tendency is a fairly reliable indicator of "permissiveness," and
it becomes relevant to note that several studies reveal a high
incidence of irreligion among the "social science" fraternity.
According to Seymour Lipset, "Studies of American religious
behavior suggest that these professors and scientists were far

more irreligious than the general population." In an associated branch of the intelligentsia—writers—a survey by James Leuba found that no less than sixty-two per cent described themselves as atheists or agnostics.

A further index to faculty permissiveness is supplied by *The Academic Mind,* previously cited. This survey of 2,451 "social scientists," at 165 American colleges, was designed to test the "permissive" or "conservative" leanings of teachers of history, economics, sociology, political science, social psychology, anthropology, and geography. Two broad categories relevant to the present inquiry—philosophy and literature—were not included; enough subjects were covered, however, to suggest that the Lazarsfeld-Thielens study comes close to representing the net predispositions of the academic community.

From a survey covering some 45 questions, the authors deduced, first, that "in most social science faculties conservative teachers were in the minority. It would seem a fair estimate to say that the over-all size of this sector of the professoriate lies somewhere between the fourteen per cent whom our index classifies as clearly conservative and the twenty-eight per cent whom it designates as at least somewhat conservative." The rest, the overwhelming majority, are "permissive" Liberals. "Irrespective . . . of one's personal predilections," they conclude, "it must be accepted as a 'fact of nature' that permissiveness characterizes the prevailing climate of opinion among social scientists in twentieth-century America."

It should be stressed that the authors reach this conclusion on the basis of *political,* not ethical, questions. Undoubtedly the respondents would have been more hesitant to come forth with "permissive" answers if the inquiry had been suspended from elementary propositions of right and wrong. Yet the high incidence of politically permissive answers leads the authors

to deeper speculations. The professors, they note, are "tolerant of other people's opinions; they can have a searching attitude regarding the current state of society and feel that their
teaching should imbue their students with a similar spirit."
They add, in a comment that is commonplace to anyone who
has heard a conventional relativist hold forth from a university
lectern:

> The social scientist faces an additional situation deriving
> from the nature of his work, which is likely to strengthen a
> basically permissive attitude. A great discovery of anthropology
> was that there are social systems completely different from ours
> and yet viable. A major contribution of historians is the idea
> that in other periods the modes of thinking and the forms of
> social relations were different than [sic] ours, and require re-
> construction for contemporary understanding. The intellectual
> task involved in these and many similar endeavors of the social
> scientist are [sic] contingent on his ability to visualize a state
> of human affairs radically different from that of today.

Thus, in the estimation of these authors, it is indeed a cultural, and therefore ethical, permissiveness, which generates
the political relativism of the academy. Again, however, we
find the Liberals unable to make the vital connection that lies
before their eyes—to understand that the geldings, once cas-
trated, cannot be fruitful. Consider the case of Charles Van
Doren, the celebrated quiz expert of the late 1950s, who was
exposed as a fraud and poseur. Two sociologists from Queens
College conducted a poll concerning the Van Doren case, and
came up with some disturbing conclusions. Of 225 students
questioned about this national scandal, a majority considered
Van Doren, not as morally reprehensible, but as a "tragic hero."
No less than eighty-six per cent were sympathetic to him, and
twenty-six per cent found nothing at all wrong with his elaborate deception. The sociologists were deeply puzzled.

So was Professor Hans Morgenthau of the University of Chicago. Noting that 650 students at Columbia, where Van Doren had taught English, had signed a petition asking that he be rehired, Morgenthau expressed bafflement at the "moral illiteracy" of the young. Professor Morgenthau and the Queens sociologists surmised that the degrading "success" ethic of the business world had somehow penetrated the academic cloister. The academy, however, cannot so easily absolve itself of the Van Doren episode; for the evidence suggests that this professor's behavior, and the student response to it, are characteristic properties of the academy itself. The students' amoral response to immorality is, after all, a letter-perfect expression of the theories propounded by their elders. The students have simply played Smerdyakov to their professors' Ivan.

In *Changing Values in College,* Philip Jacob concludes that the tendency of a college education is to nudge students into "permissiveness," to loosen the bonds of moral constraint. Although remorseful that a college education doesn't do *more* to "Liberalize" students, Jacob notes that the college experience tends to homogenize them into a common outlook, emphasizing "a free market place for ideas, based on a respect for intelligence and acceptance of a wide diversity of opinions and beliefs," rejection of "moral taboos," and "skepticism of the supernatural as a determining force in human affairs." The student tends to adopt a "Liberal attitude," refusing to "let fixed moral standards or ingrained prejudice govern his relations with other people. . . ."

A striking case in point is a book entitled *The Unsilent Generation,* edited by Dr. Otto Butz of Princeton University. The "generation" referred to is represented by eleven members of Princeton's class of 1957, who at Butz's request prepared essays concerning their views on "happiness, success, security, God, education," and so forth. Their statements about God are instructive. Essayist Number One wrote: "I figure I can be indifferent to an indifferent God. . . it is this world, not the next one, that I'm concerned with." "I seldom think of God as such," said Two, "and only pray when I am exceptionally troubled. Even when I pray, I don't consider myself to be asking for help or advice. I simply find I derive a measure of comfort and self-assurance." Number Three allowed that, in his personal philosophy, "religion plays almost no part at all." Four expressed himself as indifferent to religion, except for Catholicism, "which I regard with disgust." Six believed that God "must be a pretty nice guy," while Seven concluded that "the objective existence of God has been made irrelevant by the industrial revolution." A few of the students had retained their religious faith, although, as Number Five put it, "Princeton has been a terribly corroding influence." And Eight observed: "At Princeton, the willing initiate is taught that self-interest and disloyalty are valuable qualities, and he soon becomes proficient at varying his beliefs and purported commitments to suit the social situation at hand."

At Vassar College, the pressures toward Liberal permissiveness are, if anything, even more intense. "The effect of this training," Mary McCarthy wrote in *Holiday,* "is to make the Vassar student, by the time she has reached her junior year, look back upon her freshman self with pity and amazement. When you talk to her about life in college you will find that she sees it as a series of before and after snapshots: 'When I came to Vassar, I thought like Mother and Daddy. . . . I was conservative in my politics. . . .' With few exceptions, the trend is from the conservative to the Liberal, from the orthodox to the heterodox." And for the "few exceptions," things are not always easy. In December, 1951, Nancy Fellers, a Vassar undergraduate, was asked to write a theme concerning her beliefs, and was told the assignment would be repeated the following spring—the implication being that the beliefs might change considerably in the interval. "I believe," responded Miss Fellers, "in God, Human Dignity, and the United States of America. Next June I shall believe in God, Human Dignity, and the United States of America." In addition, Miss Fellers dispatched a letter to the school paper, defending Bill Buckley's *God and Man at Yale.* "You do not hesitate to break into print with your dangerous ideas," her teacher told her. "If something is not done, your getting through Vassar will be imperilled." Nancy Fellers ignored the threat, and failed the course. As a result, she was not allowed to graduate with her class. Her problem, commented the Vassar *Chronicle,* was that she had "closed her mind to any possibility of change."

Summarizing an attitude survey at Vassar, Jacob says: "an intensive study of the intellectual and personality development of students at Vassar revealed some 150 traits which were significantly characteristic of seniors but not of freshmen. Combined these constituted a 'Vassar Developmental Scale' which has been statistically validated." Among other traits which constituted the "development" of Vassar girls—particularly noteworthy in view of the Van Doren syndrome—were these:

The senior is more likely than the freshman to admit to conduct and attitudes contrary to conventional moral taboos concerning drinking, telling the truth, sexual propriety, and even theft. She feels people would be happier if sex experience before marriage were taken for granted in both men and women, and that in illegitimate pregnancies abortion is in many cases the most reasonable alternative. She thinks she would probably get into a movie without paying if sure she would not be seen.

As for censuring the wrong-doings of others:

The senior is not so critical as the freshman of persons who become intoxicated, who don't vote, who have intercourse before marriage, are lawbreakers, or don't take things seriously enough. She tends not to set arbitrary standards of right and wrong conduct, and judge others by them.

Jacob enters the caveat that these views "are not unanimously shared by the Vassar seniors, nor would they necessarily be representative of college seniors everywhere." But, he says, "they do indicate what is apparently the lodestone towards which the values of girls coming to Vassar are attracted."

In view of those findings at one highly-regarded college, where students are "attracted" to the "lodestone" of tolerating lawbreakers, untruthfulness, theft, abortion, and sneaking into movies, why should anyone—particularly any social scientist—be surprised at the student response to Charles Van Doren?

What, then, of the *statist* aspect of the conformity? I have cited the evidence of textbook surveys and the testimony of individual students, but I grant that these are not systematic data. The Lazarsfeld-Thielens study did not test this sector of the faculty's views, and there is no similarly comprehensive survey which does that particular job. We may, however, by indirections find directions out.

David Riesman observes that the "inner-directed" man romanticizes a government of laws and not of men; the "other-directed American, or 'inside-dopester,' romanticizes a government of men and not of laws." The classic American, in a word, is a constitutionalist; the modern conformist believes in discretionary government action. The other-directed man would therefore favor programs of government intervention in the economy; he prefers centralized power, and governmental welfare schemes, to limited government and a maximum of individual self-reliance. He would favor the programs advocated by left-of-center political parties, ranging from Marxists at one end of the spectrum to New Dealers and New Frontiersmen at the other. Thus, by assessing the political attachments of the faculty, we may approach, if only asymptotically, their aggregate views on matters of government intervention.

On this point we have at our disposal a consistent history of leftist tendency on the part of academicians—far and above the tendencies of the country at large, even when it has been heading pell-mell toward increased government intervention. Thus, in 1937, after Roosevelt's landslide victory, it was found that fifty-six per cent of the manual workers displayed pro-New Deal sentiments. The corresponding figure for social science professors was eighty-four per cent. Lazarsfeld and Thielens found, in their survey, that 1129 of their respondents classified themselves as Democrats, only 384 as Republicans. In 1948, 1229 of them had voted for Truman, 81 for Wallace, and 548 for Dewey. In 1952, the breakdown was 1414 for Stevenson, 737 for Eisenhower.

Further suggesting the collectivist attitudes of the faculty, as well as student response to them, is the survey of Harvard undergraduates referred to in Chapter I. The survey found that, by and large, students tended to adopt increasingly interventionist attitudes as they made their way through college, and that this alteration was owing to the impact of the faculty and the course material the faculty employed. "For the most part," the *Crimson* said, "the college's students did not arrive in Cambridge with these beliefs; they picked them up at Harvard. Over half admit that their political views have been strongly influenced since freshman registration, and of these, seven-tenths have changed either 'from conservative to more Liberal,' or from 'Liberal to more Liberal.' " "Lectures and assigned readings were named as the most important influences" in directing students toward these views.

"Whereas only a twelfth of Harvard's undergraduates describe their political temperament as 'radical,' " the *Crimson* reported, "over a seventh support 'full socialization of all industries': more than a fifth favor socialization of the medical profession; . . . two-thirds support such 'Welfare State' projects as social security and federal regional power development; . . . four-fifths approve of federal aid to public secondary schools; two-thirds support national health insurance, federal aid to private colleges and universities, government wage and price controls to check inflation; and half support federal financial assistance to American cultural activities."

That these attitudes toward government correspond to a decrease in individual initiative is further attested to by David Riesman, who concludes that students, as he has observed them, want "social security, not great achievements. They want approval not fame. They are not eager to develop talents that might bring them into conflict; whereas the inner-directed young person tended to push himself to the limit of his talents and beyond. Few of them suffer, like youth in an earlier age, because they are 'twenty, and so little accomplished.' " Of one group of young people, he observes: "They take whatever government gives them, including the draft, with an almost total passivity."

Riesman conducted an experiment in one of his classes to test its attitude toward self-reliance. Referring to a study of three Indian tribes—two of them aggressive and individualist (Dobu and Kwakiutl), one docile and collectivist (Pueblo)—he asked his students to suggest which one most nearly resembled contemporary American culture. The majority picked one or the other of the aggressive tribes. "Yet," Riesman comments, "when we turn to examine the culture patterns of these very students, we see little evidence either of Dobu or Kwakiutl ways."

Riesman adds: "The wealthy students go to great lengths not to be conspicuous—things are very different from the coon-coated days of the twenties. The proper uniform is one of purposeful shabbiness. In fact, none among the students except a very rare Lucullus dares to be thought uppity. . . .

"It is, moreover, not only in the virtual disappearance of conspicuous consumption that the students have abandoned Kwakiutl-like modes of life. Other displays of gifts, native or acquired, have also become subdued. A leading college swimming star told me: 'I get sore at the guys I'm competing against. Something's wrong with me. I wish I could be like X who really cooperates with the other fellows. He doesn't care so much about winning.' "

Lionel Trilling, commenting on Riesman's experiment, recalls a similar episode: "My own experience in teaching confirms this one incident in particular. For some time I had been increasingly aware that my students had no very large admiration for Stendhal's *The Red and Black,* gave it nothing like the response that it had had from my college generation. Then one day a whole class, almost all of its members gifted men, agreed in saying that they were bored by Julien Sorel and didn't like him. Bored by Julien Sorel! But didn't he, I asked, represent their own desires for pre-eminence, their own natural young ambition? They snubbed me with their answer and fixed between themselves and me the great gulf of the generations: they did not, they said, understand ambition of Julien's self-referring kind; what they wanted was decent, socially useful cooperative work to do. I felt like an aging Machiavelli among the massed secretariat of the U.N."

And William H. Whyte, labeling today's college students a

"generation of bureaucrats," quotes one authority as observing the trend among students at theological seminaries: "It is a kind of authoritarianism in reverse. Theological students today, in contrast to their fellows of twenty years ago, want 'to be told.' I have gone out of my way to ask friends who teach in seminaries of other denominations whether they have recognized the new tendency. Without exception they have told me that they find the present generation of students less inquiring of mind, more ready to accept an authority, and indeed most anxious to have it 'laid on the line.' "

In sum, the typical professor and the typical student are conformists, other-directed men eager to throw in with the *Geist* of statism. The revolution was; Liberalism is enthroned; to conform is to be Liberal. "Some of the very attitudes which might in the 1930s have marked a man as an independent thinker, and even a nonconformist," Philip Jacob concludes, "are today thoroughly conventional. What undoubtedly appears to many students' families as thoroughly unconventional thinking and behavior is the sophistication, flexibility, and social aplomb which will enable these students to get along easily with the kind of people who will be their own neighbors and associates after graduation."

Parenthetically, a special word needs to be said on a paradoxical subject—the Liberal's characteristic view of the American Communist Party. The Liberal orthodoxy is "statist," believing that the individual should be subordinate to the group. Yet the same orthodoxy is zealous in defense of "individual rights" whenever the question of Communism arises. Those who make no protest when a farmer is cozened out of his property, a businessman is pre-empted from managing his own affairs, a working man is compelled to pay tribute to a union, or an Amish elder is broken on the wheel of "social security"—those who consent to all this are the first to cry foul

when a congressional committee inquires into the fellow-trav-
elling activities of a Linus Pauling or a Cyrus Eaton. Converse-
ly, the conservative, who insists upon individual self-reliance,
generally favors such investigations. He is thus, in this instance,
characterized as an opponent of "individual rights." Do these
attitudes make sense? Or are the two sides involved in a mutual
contradiction—each abandoning its own position and adopting the arguments of the enemy? The answer, I think, is that
both sides are being quite consistent—that the confusion arises
from a rhetorical, rather than a substantive, transposition.

Within its continuum of permissive-statist ideology, Liberalism can find several adequate sanctions for its characteristic
attitude on the question of Communism. One such is an ancient
emotional commitment to Bolshevism and the Soviet Union.
As Marcus Cunliffe has observed, World War I, "along with the
Russian revolution . . . finally proved to the American *avant
garde* that they knew better than their society. It is not too wild
to say that 1917, the year of revolution and mutiny, also marked
a cultural revolution in America—a movement that was to
adopt the vocabulary of Marx together with that of Freud."
Liberals who have in milder ecstasies known the chiliastic vision
of the Marxists are hard put to abandon it.

The mood of enchantment has gone through various phases:
Liberal "intellectuals" defended Stalin's masquerade of justice in 1936; led the way in proclaiming the virtues of our
noble "Russian ally" in the early 1940s; told us that Mao Tse-
tung and Fidel Castro were "agrarian reformers"; turned up
repeatedly on the letterheads of Communist front organizations; and even today, with the Soviet record of atrocity and
dishonor graven on the mind of humanity, still entertain notions of "understanding" with the Communist enemy.

In a word, because Liberalism shared certain dirigist aspirations with the Bolsheviks, and because the Soviet Union was

the "great experiment" embodying them, it is with painful hesitation that it brings itself to believe Communism is *quite* so black as it is painted. That sentiment inevitably overflows into a distaste for congressional committees seeking to harass domestic Communists and their allies—a concern which is not apparent when, e.g., the Kefauver subcommittee sets about to red-dog wealthy businessmen.

Among conservatives these commitments are reversed. Arguing that "radical" schemes of government will not work, the conservative has nurtured a long-standing opposition to Communism and the USSR. That concern helps shape his attitude toward a particular act of our own government—derived, at several removes, from a chronically hostile disposition toward government per se—in rooting out Communists within our own society.

Such subliminal commitments, however, cannot fully explain the controversy over the question of internal Communism. On the Liberal side, the talk of "individual rights" and "civil liberties" has grown so intense and voluble that, if statist impulses are involved, they are obviously refracted and subterranean. Among conservatives, there is a similar emphasis on the point where "rights leave off," or become dangerous, and "responsibilities begin."* The rhetorical switch has been almost complete, and neither side has troubled to examine it fully, or to confess that the sanctions it invokes on this point are the reverse of those it usually employs.

The confusion arises because the contestants, Liberals and conservatives alike, speak of the Communist issue in the same rhetorical categories in which they would discuss the plight

---

* Certainly true enough in conservative theory, but a proposition which conservatives have been reluctant to have enforced by government.

of a wheat farmer who has overstepped his allotment. And this identification ignores the fact that while the farmer's troubles with government are purely a matter of internal concern, the Communist's are not. The case of the Communist, and of those who abet him, involves fealty to a foreign power, and a threat to the survival of society. The Communist runs athwart, not simply the *power* of government, but the *value* of patriotism. We thus find the two sides back in place.

Properly construed, patriotic ardor is not inconsistent with libertarian, or "inner-directed," notions about limited government. The conservative believes government has certain specified and definite functions, and those only. He expects it to perform well those tasks assigned to it, and to refrain from others. One job which without question is delegated to government—indeed, its primary responsibility—is defense against foreign enemies. The punishment of Communists falls into this category.

If I may expand upon Riesman's analysis a bit, I think our national history indicates that his "inner-directed" people profess an ascending hierarchy of secular loyalties; they revere the individual and the family vis-a-vis outside influences, the rights of the states vis-a-vis federal authority, and the rights of the United States vis-a-vis foreign enemies and supranational institutions. Each is an expression of the conservative impulse. Patriotic attachment is thus an affirmation of individuality at two removes, a pride of place enjoying intermediary status in a graduated system of affection and concern.*

In the other-directed, or Liberal, conception, the order of

---

* I acknowledge that it can become more than this, and has in given episodes—as when patriotic fervor in wartime has persuaded people to give up some of their civil liberties. But the *uses* to which patriotic emotion may be put, once it is created, do not alter the fact of its source.

priorities is inverted. Having little or no faith in the individual, the Liberal affirms the claims of the community over the person, the claims of the federal government over states, and the claims of "world opinion" or supranational institutions over the United States. Liberal anti-nationalism is part of a coherent ethic of anti-individualism.

The seemingly contradictory views on investigations of Communism thus dissolve into focus: Communists, in the conservative view, are agents of a hostile foreign power, attempting to destroy the United States. Sensing this, although not always articulating it, the conservative wants the government, his instrument of defense against foreign enemies, to take action—including action against the machinations of the enemy in our midst.

As for the Liberal, the Communist issue, I think, does not really suggest to him that our government is getting too big, or too impertinent; after all, he works night and day to manufacture a government which is precisely that. The angered nerve is that of permissiveness: the unwillingness to proscribe an exotic creed—any exotic creed; to say that in any given question one view is right, the other wrong; and hostility toward the symbol and substance of patriotic endeavor.

Thus it is that we find, comparing Samuel Stouffer's *Communism, Conformity, and Civil Liberties* with Riesman's findings, that anti-Communism is most astringent precisely in those areas where inner-direction survives (primarily the rural areas), while tolerance of Communism is highest precisely in those centers (the cities, the bureaucratic class) where other-direction is strongest. Firm anti-Communism is an expression of inner-directed commitment to tradition and value; tolerance of Communism is an expression of other-directed anomie.

That Liberal views on the Communist question are an aspect of "permissiveness" is both the assumption and the demonstrated verdict of Lazarsfeld's and Thielens' study. One question, for example, is designed to test the respondents' reaction to a hypothetical ban on a campus speaking engagement by Owen Lattimore, twice identified under oath as a member of the Communist apparatus, and branded by the Senate Internal Security subcommittee as a "conscious, articulate instrument of the Soviet conspiracy." (Facts not mentioned in the survey, but known, I trust, to most well-informed people.) No less than eighty per cent of the respondents would approve of a speech by Lattimore, and 970 of those would "protest vigorously" if the school administration were to prevent such a speech.

One thousand and one respondents believe American Communists are "some danger" to the United States (as opposed to a "very great" or "great" danger), while 859 believe domestic Communists represent "hardly any danger." Seven hundred thirty-three—almost one-third—believe a "social science teacher who is an admitted Communist" is "not very different from any other teacher with unorthodox views."

These findings correspond with those contained in the Stouffer report, which found that "tolerance" of Communism varies almost directly with exposure to the educational process. Expanding on this point, Lazarsfeld and Thielens note further: "Forty-three per cent of Stouffer's national sample considered Communism a great or very great danger, compared to fourteen per cent of our respondents. But the social scientists made finer distinctions. Six per cent of the general population would not fire a Communist in a defense plant and twenty-six per cent would allow one to continue as a clerk in a store, a difference of twenty per cent. With professors the same difference is sixty-five per cent; eighty-two per cent would not fire a Communist from a store, while *only* seventeen per cent would not eliminate him from a defense plant." [Italics added]

That professors are less apprehensive of Communism, the authors believe, "is largely due to a difference in attitudes toward unorthodox ideas." But, considering that the professors are more willing, by almost three-to-one, to keep a Communist on *in a defense plant,* it might also have something to do with a chronic inability of the Liberal mind to confront the reality of Communism. The "intolerance" of the uneducated is, though unfortunate, understandable; but what can account for the tenacious ignorance of presumably knowledgeable people, who after forty years of betrayal are so agreeable to the presence of Communists in American defense plants?

Someone has observed that the formulation of the Stouffer report makes it difficult to know when resistance to Communism comes from a true apprehension of Communist reality and when it comes from parochial bias against anything and everything "radical." By the same token, it is difficult to know when "tolerance" of Communism is based on a compassionate desire to give freedom to heretics, and when it is based on persistent blindness to the dangers confronting us. The evidence on the record, *pace* Stouffer and *The Academic Mind,* suggests that American faculties, deeply infected with ideological myopia, are willing to tolerate Communists more out of ignorance than out of enlightenment. (This point becomes particularly apposite as we move on to the next section of this chapter and examine Liberal tolerance of "heresy" which is not of the radical sort.)

Thus the reigning attitude of American faculties toward the question of internal Communism. How are they reflected in the minds of the students they have been training?

At Vassar, it was determined that the typical senior, more than the typical freshman, "questions whether 'Communism is the most hateful thing in the world today' or whether the American way of life should be preserved unchanged; would prefer to betray country rather than best friend." In a survey at Columbia, "students overwhelmingly condemned congressional investigation of colleges in principle and as currently practiced." At Columbia, UCLA, and the University of California at Berkeley, "a majority of students were found to have no categorical objections to the employment of Communists on the faculty. . . ."

The reactions of the students demonstrate once more that tolerance of Communism is intimately related to a disparaging attitude toward American sovereignty. From the survey at Antioch, Colgate, and Michigan State, it develops that students were pushed toward "a self-critical approach to the national American culture based on a recognition of world interdependence and rejection of chauvinism." Jacob says that "by the time they graduate, about three-fourths of the students across the country qualify as 'internationalists.' They declare they are willing to have a world organization make binding decisions on national governments, including their own." Similar attitudes were discovered at Harvard, where fully one-third of the student body was found to favor unilateral suspension of American nuclear tests, and surrender by the United States in preference to a world war. A majority of Cantabridgians support recognition of Communist China.

Such, then, is the conformity which prevails on American campuses. It is "permissive," anti-religious, and relativist in the realm of ethics; statist in the realm of politics; anti-anti-Communist in the *sui generis* crisis which grips our age. In a word, it is Liberal.

II

A Short Way With Dissent

WHAT IS "ACADEMIC FREEDOM" and who are its ene-
mies? Robert MacIver gives this definition, vis-a-vis the inquiring scholar: "A right claimed by the accredited educator, as
teacher and as investigator, to interpret his findings and to
communicate his conclusions without being subjected to any
interference, molestation, or penalization because these conclusions are unacceptable to some constituted authority within or
beyond the institution."

Dangers to "academic freedom" arise, *inter alia,* when prejudice encounters "heresy": "Where prejudice is the motive,"
MacIver says, "people not only believe they already possess the
truth but also are afraid of the 'heresies' of those who come to
different conclusions—afraid lest the heretics mislead or corrupt
others. They are unwilling to trust their own untested 'truth'
not only in the market place of opinions but also in the enclaves
where men are peculiarly engaged in the search for knowledge."

These, I think, are fairly representative definitions of academic freedom and the motives of those who would destroy it—
proposed by a gentleman who believes that, by and large, the
principal danger to "academic freedom" occurs when people
become alarmed about leftist tendencies on the campus.

218

"Academic freedom" is threatened, then, when a vested interest seeks to suppress intellectual dissent on the campus. But
we have seen that the principal vested interest in our society is
Liberalism, and that it is even more powerful on college campuses than elsewhere. The question then becomes, if we are
truly concerned with "academic freedom": How does this vested
interest dispose itself toward dissent?

As we have noted, Liberals are quite willing, as a matter of
doctrine, to let "radicals" and even pro-Communists remain
on the faculty—as witness the case of Owen Lattimore; to
welcome outside speakers who have been implicated in Communist enterprises—or even acknowledged Communists—as witness the cordial reception afforded to John Gates at Columbia,* or Alger Hiss at Princeton; to tolerate aberrant outbursts
by radical students—as witness the reception given on various
campuses to the Castro-financed "Fair Play For Cuba" committee. "Academic freedom" also forbids discourtesies towards
Communists, or fellow travellers, or those who have become
mired in mistaken policies toward Communism. Thus, in the
donnybrook surrounding the late Senator McCarthy, Liberals
insisted that we must, in the interests of civility, treat our opponents fairly no matter how much we might disagree with
them.

Among faculty and undergraduates who partake of the Liberal conformity, these views are urged with passionate energy.
So far—given the premises of "academic freedom" and "dissent"
—so good. But the Liberal orthodoxy disposes itself somewhat
differently toward *conservative* dissent. "The Liberal consensus
within the intellectual community," Seymour Lipset observes,
"has served to intimidate conservatives much more than outside

* At the time he was invited to speak at Columbia, John Gates was still
editor of the *Worker.*

prying and criticism has inhibited those left-of-center." Ludwig Lewisohn of Brandeis says: "The only scholar, the only type of student who is still forced into a defensive position on American campuses today is the conservative teacher or student, the religious teacher or student."

Thus it happens that, where Liberals rule—and that is practically everywhere—conservatives, in Morton Cronin's description, have kept "their conservatism to themselves, satisfied with the occasional statement that they are not ashamed of being black."

Case histories to document such statements are not wanting. Consider the experience of Father Hugh Halton, former chaplain to Catholic students at Princeton University. In the spring of 1956, Princeton demonstrated its fealty to "academic freedom" by making university facilities available to the unrepentant Communist, Alger Hiss, who held forth to Nassau students on the nuances of American foreign policy. Father Halton had protested. He had similarly spoken out concerning the advisability of appointing J. Robert Oppenheimer, physicist and eminent security risk, as "William James" lecturer at Harvard, and of allowing John Gates, then editor of the Communist *Worker*, to speak at Columbia. As if this were not enough to exhaust the patience of the most impassive Liberal, Halton had conducted a running battle with several members of the Princeton faculty, who were variously engaged in propounding atheism and anti-Catholicism to Princeton students. For these cumulative reasons, Princeton barred Father Halton from exercising the privileges of chaplain, and severed his connection with the University. No bill of particulars was submitted, beyond the comment that the priest was guilty of "irresponsible attacks upon the intellectual integrity of faculty members."

But Father Halton, in decrying the atheism and the anti-

Catholicism of these faculty members, had largely confined his indictment to quotation from the works of those indicted. President Goheen's statement did not specify what portions of Father Halton's bill of particulars was in error. Without such specifics, backed by adequate refutation, Father Halton's case, on the face of it, was not only convincing but devastating.

It can hardly be alleged against Father Halton that he was much more than a conservative gadfly—a source of controversy, perhaps, and, at worst, of intellectual dissension. But is that not, after all, a desideratum of "academic freedom"? Certainly Father Halton was no more responsible for dissension than were his adversaries, promulgating doctrines necessarily offensive to Catholic students in the Princeton community. (Recall the statements of the Princeton seniors concerning religion.) Clearly, the major crime committed by Father Halton was that he provoked controversy by *resisting* offensive doctrines—much as, in Walter Reuther's view, the Kohler Company was culpable for UAW violence by not submitting to Reuther's demands, or as, in Khrushchev's opinion, the United States is responsible for "world tensions" by not conceding the globe to Moscow. In a word, Father Halton's offense was that he spoke militantly for religious conviction, and in so doing outraged the prevailing conformity.

Similar episodes have been enacted on many American campuses, in which conservative spokesmen have found themselves isolated, ostracized, and finally forced off the faculty. E. Merrill Root sums up several such episodes in his book, *Collectivism on the Campus,* supplying extensive documentation of the Liberal urge to extinguish conservative dissent. A particularly noteworthy case involved a conflict at Massachusetts Institute of Technology between two professors—one a knowledgeable anti-Communist, and the other an identified member of the Communist Party. These were, respectively, Dr. Alexander St. Ivanyi, a popular teacher of political science, and Professor Dirk J. Struik, an equally popular professor of mathematics. Professor Struik had been identified by Herbert Philbrick, the FBI counterspy, as a teacher at the Communist Samuel Adams School in Boston, and as a member of a Communist Party cadre. Others subsequently confirmed the identification. In 1951, Struik was indicted under the Anti-Anarchy Law of Massachusetts, and a seething controversy developed around the case. As various Liberals labored to exonerate Struik, Dr. St. Ivanyi undertook to comment. He had observed, he said, that Struik, even though a teacher of mathematics, had been able to persuade some of his students to a pro-Soviet point of view. "It is an every day occurrence," he observed, "that the excellence of a person in one particular field is accepted by their admirers as meaning an excellence in every field."

Such were the two sides in the dispute; Professor Struik, the professor identified as a Communist; Professor St. Ivanyi, the anti-Communist teacher who spoke out against him. How did M.I.T. treat these two combatants?

Toward Dr. Struik, the university acted with tender lenience. First it conducted its own investigation, and found Struik to be above reproach. Then, when he was indicted, it suspended him from teaching, but kept him on the university payroll. When the Supreme Court in 1956 struck down the various state sedition laws, Dr. Struik was returned to full status on the faculty. "We are not a legal body with powers of trying or conducting a case," commented the M.I.T. administration. "If the authorities cannot find suitable charges, it seems hardly our role to do so."

Dr. St. Ivanyi was not dealt with so gently. In the aftermath of the controversy, he was informed that his services would no longer be required at M.I.T. The stated reason was a reduction in staff, in which Dr. St. Ivanyi was deemed expendable. This in spite of the fact that the head of his department said: "Students have crowded his section to the point where some have had to be sent to other instructors."

Father Halton and Dr. St. Ivanyi were not the only anti-Communists to suffer a sudden loss of employment. Another experiencing this difficulty was William T. Couch, who ran afoul of Dr. Robert Maynard Hutchins. Hutchins has put himself on record rather nobly with regard to academic freedom. "The danger to our institutions," he declaimed to an Illinois investigating committee in 1949, "is not from the tiny minority who do not believe in them. It is from those who would mistakenly repress the free spirit upon which those institutions are built. The policy of repression of ideas cannot work and never has worked."

When it suited his purposes, however, Hutchins was not above giving that policy a try. And as Dr. Couch can testify, up to a certain point, it "worked"— since it separated Dr. Couch from his job as head of the University of Chicago Press. Dr. Couch, we must note, had made certain mistakes—principally the mistake of criticizing American universities for their laggard performance in recognizing the dangers of Communism. Such opinions were not likely to please Hutchins, who had proclaimed that anti-Communist investigations, not Communism, represented "the greatest menace to the United States since Hitler."

After ventilating his anti-Communist opinions, and publishing some books of similar tendency, Dr. Couch was notified that he was finished at Chicago. He was given little more than six hours to vacate his office—a dismissal so abrupt that a faculty subcommittee investigating the episode termed it a "gross violation of the rights normally accorded to members of the academic community." The circumstances, the subcommittee added, "clearly implied the action was being taken on statutory ground of 'inadequate performance of duties and misconduct.' We who have had access to the documents and testimony bearing on the case know that there has been no slightest suggestion of misconduct. . . . No hearings were held prior to the dismissal nor did Mr. Couch have any opportunity to defend himself on charges of inadequate performance of duties. . . . To this extent we regard the dismissal as a violation of tenure."

It is interesting to note that in none of these cases—Halton, St. Ivanyi, or Couch—did the usual spokesmen for "civil liberties," so far as diligent inquiry can determine, utter a solitary word of protest. These are only three of innumerable such episodes on the record; those involving Felix Wittmer, Anthony Bouscaren, Charles Callan Tansill, Kenneth Colegrove, Frank Richardson, A. H. Hobbs, and numerous others might be recited at length.

Conservative students have, from time to time, been subjected to similar pressures—as the case of Nancy Fellers at Vassar well demonstrated. Patricia Bozell, a Vassar alumna, recalls the experience of another student, Micheline Peon, who wrote a paper criticizing the presidential candidacy of Henry Wallace. The teacher, the same teacher who had failed Nancy Fellers, was so angered that she returned the paper, Mrs. Bozell relates, by literally throwing it in Miss Peon's face. Miss Peon, a graduate of the Sorbonne, asked if she were being judged on her work or on her ideas. The teacher's answer: "On your ideas." Miss Peon had also written a newspaper story reflecting unfavorably on the Wallace candidacy and its partisans. The teacher, reports Mrs. Bozell, accused Miss Peon of "resorting to yellow journalism. She added excitedly that Miss Peon had 'been had,' and suggested that she might do better to return to France."

At Harvard, the self-proclaimed citadel of "academic freedom," conservative students have run into similar difficulties. In 1957 Harvard exhibited its devotion to free inquiry by appointing Dr. J. Robert Oppenheimer as its "William James Lecturer." From the proceedings in which Oppenheimer had lost his security clearance with the Atomic Energy Commission, it was learned that he had contributed money to the Communist Party until 1942, associated with known Communists, and lied to a security officer (all of which, under cross-examination, he admitted). This record, the conservative students believed, raised some few questions as to Oppenheimer's fitness to lecture on matters of philosophy and ethics. They decided to sponsor a public debate on the subject, "Should Oppenheimer Be James Philosophy Lecturer at Harvard?" To state the case against Oppenheimer they secured Dr. Medford Evans, for eight years an official of the Atomic Energy Commission; and Professor Willmoore Kendall, former Professor of Political Science at Yale University. Defending Oppenheimer were attorney Howard S. Whiteside, counsel for the American Civil Liberties Union, and Dr. Chase Kimball, also affiliated with the ACLU and former law professor at Boston University. The lecture hall was crowded with students and townspeople; it was a rousing debate, thoroughly enjoyed by all concerned. Its most significant feature, however, was not so much in what took place that evening, as the attitude taken toward the proceedings by the Harvard administration.

It is important to note that the students engaged in this enterprise were merely trying to provide a forum in which *both sides* of a highly controversial problem could be ventilated—the

kind of dialogue which, according to their own mythology, Liberal academicians insist should take place in our universities.
The Oppenheimer debate gave them ample occasion to demonstrate their loyalty to that principle. But what in fact happened?

To begin with, the students encountered numberless ob-
stacles in obtaining University facilities for the program—so
many, in fact, that they finally held it in a privately-owned
building on the University grounds. Moreover, the leaders of
the conservative group found themselves arraigned by Harvard
officialdom. William C. Brady II, who took a leading role in
arranging for the debate, recalls:

> The next move was for the Dean's office to call in several of
> the officers and a former officer separately. They were ques-
> tioned closely. They were asked questions about each other—
> some of them of a highly personal nature. They were questioned
> closely as to the financial sources of the club, and who or what
> group was financing the debate. (Answer: the funds came from
> individual alumni sympathetic to our cause, personal contri-
> butions from students, and the club treasury. . . .) They were
> questioned again, and even more closely, about the proposed
> participants.
> The spokesman and past officer of the club, who had appeared
> on the John Daly national television news program with some
> other students and criticized the appointment of Oppenheimer
> (although in measured language), was singled out for the longest
> session of all. He didn't mind; I know, for the student who
> stood longest on the carpet was myself. Being called to account
> for conservative agitation was only to be expected.

Under questioning by the Dean, Brady stood his ground. "I
was told by the Dean of Students Activities," he adds, "that
appearing on Daly's TV program was 'extremely dangerous.'
In fact, he said, I was 'playing with fire.' It was suggested that
such behavior was grounds for expulsion . . . 'conduct unbecom-

ing a Harvard student.' I was informed further than another dean had been in the office and had emphatically stated that 'something should be done' about the trouble-makers, and that he had suggested that the matter be taken up that afternoon at the weekly Faculty Committee meeting."

The debate at last was held, but not without further repercussions. A few days prior to that meeting, one of the club's two faculty advisers resigned. On the evening of the debate, the second withdrew, alleging that the proceedings were "discourteous" to Dr. Oppenheimer. Since the Harvard Rules and Regulations Governing Undergraduate Organizations require that a group have official advisers to maintain a charter, the existence of the club was finally threatened. It finally resorted to asking two alumni to serve in that capacity—a step permissible under University Rules. Later, when the conservatives launched a new undergraduate magazine, the *Harvard Fortnightly,* they ran into the same problem.

Again, although the academic community is eager to make its facilities available to outside speakers of all persuasions, including Communists like Alger Hiss and John Gates, it is reluctant to extend the same courtesy to anti-Communist speakers. One of the most peculiar exercises of this double standard occurred not long ago at the University of Detroit, a Jesuit school. Two young conservatives named George McDonnell and Mary Ann Krasusky have activated a vigorous conservative movement there. In addition to serving as Michigan State Chairman for Young Americans for Freedom, McDonnell did a stint as President of the Young Republican Club. In the fall of 1960, he sought to bring William F. Buckley, Jr. to the Detroit campus as a speaker before the YRs. Buckley's projected topic was, appropriately enough, "The Superstitions of Academic Freedom." The request was refused.

The given reason is so strange an inversion of logic as to suggest that the age of newspeak and doublethink is indeed upon us. Wayne State University, a Liberal stronghold in Detroit, had recently lifted a ban on Communist speakers. To have Buckley come to Detroit and speak harshly of "academic freedom," the authorities reasoned, would be interpreted as a "hostile act" toward Wayne State. In other words, in order to have academic freedom for Communists at Wayne State, academic freedom for anti-Communists must be extinguished at the University of Detroit!

A somewhat parallel episode transpired in New Haven in the summer of 1957. The Yale Divinity School, meeting place of the Central Committee of the World Council of Churches, had opened its gates to several alleged "clergymen" representing Communist slave regimes of Eastern Europe. (Among the Central Committeee's Iron Curtain members were Professor Josef Hromadka of Czechoslovakia, and Bishop Lajos Veto, a member of the Communist Hungarian Parliament.)

Anti-Communist ministers belonging to the American Council of Christian Churches sought to gather in New Haven to protest this traffic with Communists under the guise of "religion." A spokesman for the group explained: "We want the people behind the Iron Curtain to know that there are Christians in the United States that do not accept this collaboration and so-called peaceful coexistence in the churches which Hromadka preaches and the World Council of Churches preaches."

From any informed view of the Communist danger, this declaration not only made sense, but represented an eloquent affirmation of moral purpose. But the Yale administration, instead of extending to the anti-Communist ministers the same courtesy it showed the representatives of Soviet slavery, denied them the use of any and all university facilities. The reason: the proposed protest meeting was "controversial." Additionally, a representative of the Yale administration referred to the anti-Communist ministers as a "gangster" organization—a sardonic twist which the enslaved people of Hungary, Poland, and East Germany would no doubt find amusing.

The anti-Communist ministers, who hunted up other facilities for their meeting, offered this comment: "Yale is a private institution. There is no law that compels it to give one of its halls to either the World Council or the American Council. However, since Yale University talks about academic freedom . . . it ought to practice what it preaches. It ought to demonstrate to the world that it believes that the freedom it talks about can be exercised even on the Yale campus. But the truth is that this vaunted Liberalism is not so liberal. It will discriminate and suppress a conservative group that has strong convictions about including Communists in Christian fellowship."

We came, finally, to the matter of "fairness" in regard to one's opposition—to the Liberal's aversion to "McCarthyism," the term he identifies with incivilities in political discourse. Over the past several months, I have had occasion to appear on a number of college campuses in conjunction with the documentary film, "Operation Abolition." Invariably, to my observation, Liberal viewers have greeted it with rank discourtesy—shouting, cheering, laughing uproariously during the course of it, and in general doing everything within their power to destroy its effectiveness through ridicule. In speaking in its defense, I have found its opponents possessed by that species of irrationality which will brook no disagreement, and which attempts to shout down its adversaries rather than to reason with them.

On other occasions, I have encountered displays of rude-

ness beside which Dr. Johnson would have been taken for an
Elizabethan courtier. In one episode, after a speech at Antioch
College, I had the experience of having a student editor refer
to me as a "fascist"—an allegation which drew the censure of the
school's Civil Liberties Subcommittee, but for which the campus Publications Board and the Antioch administration felt no
apology or retraction was necessary.

In sum, all the courtesies that the Liberal conformity insists
be extended to Communists—the right to remain on the faculty,
the right of outsiders to use university facilities, the right of
activist students to indulge their enthusiasm, and the right to
a fair hearing without abuse—are pointedly withheld from conservative dissenters.

Indeed, as Professor MacIver said, "where prejudice is the
motive, people not only believe they already possess the truth
but also are afraid of the 'heresies' of those who come to different conclusions—afraid lest the heretics mislead or corrupt
others." Amen, and amen.

III

Freedom for Conservatives

THE FOREGOING ARGUMENT is meant to establish that Liberalism is the orthodoxy on American campuses, and that, in many recorded instances, it has sought to repress conservative dissent; that, in fact, it violates its own high-sounding conception of "academic freedom."

Most discussions of this subject choose to ignore such facts, and thus have about them an aura of hallucination. The outcries against "thought control" by such as Chancellor Hutchins, when they are themselves exercising thought control, bear so little connection with reality that no rational discussion may be premised upon them.

There have been, however, some divagations on "academic freedom" which are based on the facts as they actually exist. These have developed into a sort of triangular debate involving William F. Buckley, Jr., Sidney Hook, and Russell Kirk. Examination of the principal point raised in this discussion will, I think, illuminate the problems of "academic freedom," and supply an appropriate coda for this essay.

Bill Buckley launched the debate in *God and Man at Yale,*

which was subtitled "The Superstitions of Academic Freedom."
He argued, as I have, that what goes under the name of "academic freedom" is in reality a massive pressurization process,
conditioning students to accept atheism (what I have called
permissiveness) and collectivism (what I have called statism). In
casting about for an alternative to this process, Buckley decided
that the alumni and the parents, who pay the bills for the
colleges and universities, should have something to say. On the
premise that the buyer should get what he wants for his money,
Buckley concluded that the alumni ought to rise up against the
Liberalizing pressures exerted by Yale. If they want their sons
to be indoctrinated in free enterprise and Christianity, he reasoned, they should have exactly that. The relationship was that
of buyer and seller, purely contractual.

Sidney Hook, in *Heresy Yes—Conspiracy No,* undertook to
challenge Buckley's thesis. The alumni and the parents, he argued, regardless of their contractual rights in the matter, are
not competent to know what is good pedagogy and what is not.
Inquiry, he argues, can be limited only by "the compulsions of
evidence." Buckley's position "is comparable to saying that because every man has a right to eat what he pleases, therefore he
is as good an authority on food values as any other, and that it
is undemocratic to recognize experts."

And Russell Kirk, joining the discussion in his book, *Academic Freedom,* similarly paraphrased Buckley's position:
"When Mr. Buckley, then, demands that boards of trustees, and
alumni associations, exact a conformity to certain doctrines
from all scholars and teachers, I am afraid that he must take
the position that persons outside the academy know more about
what the academy ought to do than persons inside the academy;
and I think this position is untenable."

Indeed, the position suggested by these remarks would be

untenable; but it is not, on my reading, Buckley's position. *God and Man at Yale,* by invoking the metaphor of commercial exchange, does not argue that alumni are experts in the science of instruction, any more than a free market economist would argue that car-owners are experts in the art of manufacturing automobiles. Yet consumer preference is what dictates the mode and style of the automobile, and what determines whether automobile companies prosper or do not. The point is not whether the consumer is familiar with the processes of production; it is whether he has a right to *assess the end-product,* and to decide whether it is worth the price he is asked to pay for it. This is all that Buckley urges: that the alumni, who pay the bills, ought to have some right to appraise the services for which the bills are rendered—the kind of minds being turned out by Yale University. If they are aghast at the sort of mind resulting from the educational process there, they certainly have the right to withdraw their support. And the threat of that withdrawal, if sufficiently strong and sufficiently real, will of course have some bearing on whether the process is altered.

At one point, Buckley uses a formulation which, upon casual reading, would suggest active participation of the alumni in shaping the curriculum. ". . . in the last analysis," he writes, "academic freedom must mean the freedom of men and women to supervise the educational activities and aims of the schools they oversee and support." "Supervise" implies the kind of activity which Kirk and Hook believe Buckley wants. But it is clear enough in context that Buckley's real goal is to have education policies "supervised" as *consumers* "supervise" any commodity—by directing productive activity into one channel or another through shifts in demand, allocating dollars at one point, withholding them at another.

In the peroration of his book, he says:

My final point is that alumni and friends cannot support an institution that encourages values they consider inimical to the public welfare if they wish to be honest in their convictions and faithful to the democratic tradition. . . . Preliminary to endowing . . . future leaders of this country, we have some obligation to speculate as to the direction in which they will lead us.

I shall be plainer and more specific. If the majority of Yale graduates believe in spiritual values and in individualism, they cannot contribute to Yale so long as she continues in whole or in part to foster contrary values. I go even farther. If the majority of Yale's governing body [the Yale Corporation] elected to narrow the existing orthodoxy along the lines I have sketched, I should not expect that the minority of the alumni who believe atheism and socialism to be values superior to religion and capitalism, could in good conscience continue to support Yale.

Then:

. . . should the administration of Yale recast her educational attitude and make a conscientious effort to imbue her students with those values that her educational overseers [the alumni] cherish, she ought never to want for support. . . . Her alumni could not afford not to support to the limit of their resources an institution of demonstrated efficacy, devoted to the preservation of our civilization.

It is quite apparent from this that the Yale corporation and the Yale administration would be expected to supervise the redirection of the curriculum, just as General Motors and its management staff would recast an automobile design. The alumni perform, in this metaphor, as the consumers, the *ultimate* judges, whose dollar ballots for this or that end-product—collectivism or free enterprise, Packards or Volkswagons—guide the decisions of these specialized intermediaries.

On theoretical grounds, it is hard to reject Buckley's argument. Why should education—a service infinitely more important than thousands of others purveyed in a free society—be relegated to a coterie of "experts," and sealed away from the values and the aspirations of those who are paying for it? We are unceasingly told that the free market place is the best arena for establishing the validity of ideas. Why not let the alumni, the actual consumers, participate in that market?

Nor can there be much question that the situation we have canvassed is one which should concern the alumni. The conditions described above not only violate the classic values of the American tradition; they have demonstrably weakened American society.*

The question then becomes: What is the *best* course for intervention? Buckley argues that, since the colleges are instruments of the community, they should serve to perpetuate community values—the Western legacy of Christian virtue and personal freedom. In short, to reverse the process from indoctrination in Liberal orthodoxy to indoctrination (suitably qualified) in conservative orthodoxy. In Buckley's hypothetical

---

* During the Korean conflict, more captured Americans "went over to the enemy" than ever before in history. In determining why, various experts found the same erosion of value which had marked the reaction to Van Doren. Edward Hunter, who invented the term "brainwashing" and who has made an extensive study of the problem, says:

"The main vulnerabilities that the Reds were able to exploit in their victims are frequently glamorized here in America as a misnamed 'liberal education,' an extremist 'seeing the other fellow's point of view,' watching out only for 'What's in it for me?' and a host of other supposedly 'modern traits' that brand anything as 'corny' that wasn't strictly new."

Hunter's observations are seconded by Major William E. Mayer, the Army psychiatrist who examined returning soldiers who had been brainwashed. "The behavior of many Americans in Korean prison camps, appears," Mayer said, "to raise serious questions about American character, and about the education of Americans." The typical brainwashee, he added, "was an individual who based his sense of security and often of superiority on transient, materialistic values, and was a man who, if deprived of material sources of support, would prove to be insecure, easily manipulated and controlled, lacking in real loyalties and convictions."

college, the faculty would examine a number of points of view, but would *advocate* only one—the conservative. The advocacy would be necessarily delicate, and would consist in demonstrating the merits of, say, Burke, in comparison with the fallacies of Auguste Comte. But even though the alumni have the *right* to demand education in this vein, would they be wise to enforce it? For an answer, we must have some opinion about the purpose of the academy.

The leading premise of education in the West—subject to considerable modification in recent years—is that the academy exists to discipline the intellectual faculties, to impart certain elements of expertise, and to endow the educated with certain habits of mind. In courses possessing an inherent system of discipline—mathematics, sciences, languages—these steps are accomplished out of necessity. Unless a fairly rigorous turn of mind is cultivated, the student is incapable of absorbing the subject matter.

The area in which these particular ends of education have become obscured—and the area in which the dispute over "academic freedom" has been most heated—is the "liberal arts" curriculum. In such courses as literature, history, the social sciences, philosophy, or political theory, the subject matter is not suspended from a structure of formal reasoning. They lend themselves to discursive presentation, in which questions of value necessarily arise. Because of their indefinite character, there is abroad a conception of the "liberal arts" which grants them two functions only: to impart substantive knowledge, and to suggest value judgments concerning that knowledge. Thus a course in English literature, in examining Milton or Tennyson, will at some point contain reference to metrics and the technical aspects of the manipulation of language. But it will perforce move to a consideration of excellence, or the lack of it, in the matter under study—concerning technical execution, aesthetic impact, substantive content.

It is precisely at this point that the opinions of the teacher become most effective in shaping those of his students. Value judgments rendered incidental to analysis of a poem—say, one of Wordsworth's patriotic sonnets—arise easily enough, and tend to be accepted as just as much a matter of expertise as the technical critique. The instructor's mantle of authority extends to matters in which he may be no more competent than the students to whom he lectures; but because he knows the technical aspects of his subject, his opinions on questions of value assume an irrelevant prestige.

The point becomes more obvious in matters of history, sociology, political science, or philosophy, where value judgments are an integral part of the instruction. Surveying the debates of Gladstone and Disraeli, the mores of Muncie, Indiana, the progress of the French Revolution, or the ethic of Bentham, the professor encounters myriad opportunities where he not only can, but must, enter into matters of political philosophy.

With his professors unanimously stressing the Liberal view of things at every such opening, the tractable student is necessarily influenced to accept that view. This, then, is the breach through which the Liberal professoriate has poured its army of relativist-collectivist ideas, and it is through this same breach that Buckley would thrust the conservative counterattack.

Both sorts of indoctrination begin from the premise that, because the liberal arts have no intrinsic system of discipline, their function is simply to transmit information and certain opinions concerning it. This is, for all their rhetoric, the position held by the Liberals now in charge of American education. (Thus, as Professor Raymond English observes, we find James Conant suggesting that the purpose of the liberal arts curriculum is to provide training in "democracy" and in the art of "adjusting" to the world around us.) And it is, *mutatis mutandis,* the position held by Bill Buckley: "the education overseer is paying for the transmission of knowledge [facts] and values [opinions]."

This sort of controversy, I think, begs the question of whether the liberal arts can or should perform any function beyond the flat transmission of fact and attitude. For there is a further school of thought—imperfectly suggested by Liberal oratory—which holds that the liberal arts can *train* the mind, as well as furnish it with the properly certified abstractions. Which holds, that is, that the liberal arts have to themselves a form of intellectual discipline which teaches the student *how* to think, as well as what to think.

Through education the student acquires habits of mind enabling him to achieve truth through intellection. The educated mind is capable of discriminating among ideas—of reaching past simplistic formulae and grasping the complex fabric of wisdom. It is capable of perceiving distinctions, degree, homology, contrast; and, from that mature exercise, of emerging, not with the notion that things are too complicated for understanding, but with a clear perception of what is valid and durable, of what is wrong and trivial. The educated sensibility must hold compresent the diarchic imperatives of clear thought: to perceive variety and order alike—order arising from the inherent rhythms of variety, variety functioning within the theoretical patterns of order.

The end of reason, Whitehead wrote, is "the enjoyment of contrasts within the scope of method." It is this fusion of discipline and receptivity—the rigor of intellection and the opening of the mind to nuance and degree—which leads to truth, and which gives truth the subjective power of conviction. And a student cannot attain it, or approach it, if his "education" consists simply in getting by heart a set of facts and opinions. Both are subjectively meaningless unless derived from the growth of conviction, and construed against the fabric of thought which produced it. "A thought that is separated from the mental road that leads toward it," said Ortega, "a thought standing alone and abrupt as an island, is an abstraction in the worst sense of the word, and by the same token is unintelligible."

Thus the liberal arts can and should, as Cardinal Newman believed, establish a "philosophical habit of mind." And that habit is achieved through exposure to, and participation in, the competition among disciplines and among ideas. The ideal university, in Newman's view, was "an assemblage of learned men, zealous for their own sciences, and rivals of each other . . . brought, by familiar intercourse and for the sake of intellectual peace, to adjust together the claims and relations of their respective subjects of investigation." In such a concourse of ideas, he concluded, there "is created a pure and clear atmosphere of thought, which the student also breathes. . . ."

Thus the case for free inquiry, rather than indoctrination; for the interchange and competition of ideas, rather than the reign of orthodoxy. And such a dialectic cannot be achieved, however "objective" the instructors, if the stewards of the academy all hold to a single point of view. The canons of inquiry demand that many points of view be represented, and that all be given free expression.

I realize that such sentiments, when voiced by Liberal proponents of "academic freedom," are thought to dispose of Buckley's critique. But they in fact vindicate the main thrust of his argument. For what Buckley demonstrates, as do the other data we have reviewed, is that free inquiry is precisely what we do *not* have now on American campuses. Instead, we have a machine for molding students into acceptance of Liberal values. There is no true dialectic between ideas; there is only a fugue in which associated strains of thought are contrapunted in the feeblest simulacrum of argument.

Liberal thinking, as it prevails on the American campus, demonstrates neither the pure line of disciplined thought nor the openness of honest inquiry. It is brazenly inconsistent, and meanly intolerant of dissent. And, with it all, it is destroying, rather than advancing, the primary values of our civilization.

So, under Liberalism's aegis, both ends of education are lost: The truths of the West are not imparted to the students, but are rather ridiculed. In their place, values alien to our tradition are imposed. And the intellectual strength gained by foraging among alternatives is forfeited in the absence of inquiry.

In these circumstances, conservatives have compelling reasons, tactical and substantive, to demand real fidelity to the course of free inquiry. It should be apparent that, as a tiny minority among American faculties, they are in no position to demand a total reversal from Liberal indoctrination to conservative indoctrination. Nor would they, if the foregoing discussion is valid, be well advised to do so.

But by demanding simply a *fair hearing,* given the present imbalance, they could make considerable progress. The reigning orthodoxy claims to abhor "indoctrination." Why then should not conservatives argue along the lines suggested by Peter Viereck—You profess to favor free inquiry, why not let it take place? Why not make room for some spokesmen representing the conservative alternative? Thus put, the challenge becomes an ideological embarrassment to the left, and offers no pretext for spurious discursions on the imagined iniquities of the right. As Raymond Aron observes, "they cannot dismiss criticisms derived from doctrines which they themselves invoke."

Beyond this, free inquiry should be desired as an end in itself, because it is free inquiry alone that can insure—not simply that the values of the West will gain a hearing—but that the "educated" will have the conceptual sophistication necessary to perceive and defend them. Through real "academic freedom," with all alternatives aired and examined, we may restore the American university to its proper role in the training of the intellect and the finer discipline of the spirit. And thus can we assure that ordering of thought and of marshalled conviction that is the patrimony of the West, and may be the saving of it still.

INDEX

Index

California, University of, 53, 217
Campaigne, Jameson G., Jr., 181
Carleton College, 70
Case, Sen. Clifford, 113
Castro, Fidel, 148, 211, 219
Caxton Printers, 59, 169
Cerny, Dr. Karl, 68
Chamberlain, John, 42n, 59-60
Chamberlin, William Henry, 59
Chambers, Whittaker, 59
Chiang Kai-shek, 122
Chicago, University of, 62, 67, 70-71, 89, 167, 173, 174, 176-177, 202, 223-224
Chodorov, Frank, 6, 17, 60, 63-66, 68-69, 72, 177
Claremont College, 79
Clark, Sen. Joseph, 26
Clark College, 78
Claus, Roger, 167, 176
Clemson, 158
Coldren, J. David, 32, 196
Colegrove, Kenneth, 224
Colgate, 217
Colorado School of Mines, 67
Colorado, University of, 158-159
Columbia, 79, 172, 203, 217, 219, 220
Colvin, Tom, 110
Comte, Auguste, 236
Conant, James, 237-238
Copeland, Greg, 175, 196
Cornell University, 33, 192
Couch, Dr. William T., 223-224
Coulter, Dr. Charles, 66
Courtemanche, Miss Annette, 37, 68, 174
Courtney, Kent, 96n
Courtney, Phoebe, 96n
Cowan, Richard, 110
Croll, Robert, 89-93, 97, 109
Cronin, Morton, 220
Crumpet, Peter, 174
Cunliffe, Marcus, 211
Curtis, Prof. L. P., 7
Cushing, Ned, 130, 133

Dalgetty, Bill, 37, 153-154
Daly, John, 226
Davidson College, 79, 110
Davis, Forrest, 60
Davis, Cong. James, 173

Davis, Merrill, 128
Decas, George, 9n, 45-46
Defiance College, 79
Del Mar College, 172
De Maria, Bob, 41
Dempsey, Stan, 158-159
Dennis, Bill, 192
DePauw University, 69, 71, 158, 175, 180, 196
Derham, Richard, 37
DeToledano, Ralph, 59, 97, 98
Detroit, University of, 32, 158, 227-228
    College of Law, 78
Devin-Adair, 6, 59
Dewey, Thomas E., 26, 127-129, 207
Didion, Joan, 170
Dodd, Sen. Thomas, 117n
Doob, Leonard, 63
Dos Passos, John, 17
Drake, Robert Y., 170
Driver, Cecil, 5
Dubinsky, David, 63
Duke University, 171
Dunbarton College, 158, 159

Earlham College, 69, 182, 192
Eastman, Max, 17, 59-60
Eaton, Cyrus, 211
Eckland, John, 178
Edman, V. R., 79
Edson, Peter, 104
Edwards, Lee, 109, 171, 193
Edwards, Robert, 32
Edwards, Willard, 171
Egan, Roberta, 175
Eisenhower, Dwight D., 19, 91, 127-130, 132, 148-149, 150, 207
English, Prof. Raymond, 74, 237
Evans, Dr. Medford, 225
Evjue, William, 38

Fannin, Gov. Paul, 100-101, 102
Farabee, Ray, 149
Fauber, R. E., 137
Faulkner, Harold, 63
Fellers, Nancy, 204-205, 224
Fey, Pres. John T., 79
Forster, E. M., 13
Fowler, George, 172
Franke, David, 77, 83-84, 89, 109, 116-118, 167, 173, 174, 181